COACHING·YOUNG·ATHLETES

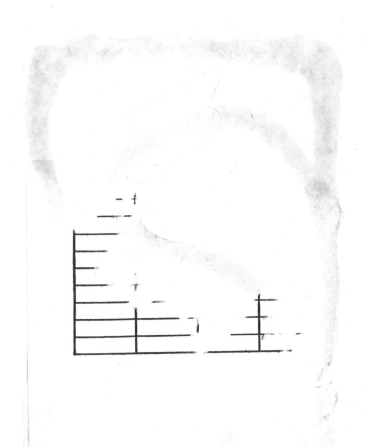

COACHING YOUNG ATHLETES

Rainer Martens, Ph.D.

Robert W. Christina, Ph.D.

John S. Harvey, Jr., M.D.

Brian J. Sharkey, Ph.D.

Human Kinetics Publishers, Inc.
Champaign, Illinois

Publications Director
Richard Howell

Copy Editor
Margery Brandfon

Typesetters
Carol Luckenbill and Cathryn Kirkham

Text Design and Layout
Denise Peters

Cover Design and Layout
Jack Davis

Library of Congress Catalog Number: 81-82451

ISBN: 0-931250-24-2

9 8 7 6 5 4 3

Human Kinetics Publishers, Inc.
Box 5076
Champaign, Illinois 61820

Table of Contents

Foreword

An estimated 12 to 15 million young athletes participate in organized youth sports in the United States. As a group these young people represent one of our country's most important resources. As individuals they are their parents' most valued possessions.

Yet all too often we as sport administrators and parents casually entrust our sons and daughters to men and women who, as research has shown, have a tremendous impact on our children's lives. The ramifications of this practice have come to haunt youth sports programs over the last decade. Now, as never before, there is an outcry for trained, competent coaches of youth sports.

Filling the void of meaningful educational materials for coaches, parents, and sport administrators is *Coaching Young Athletes*. This book, written by four of the country's leading experts in sport psychology, sport physiology, sport pedagogy, sports medicine, and sport administration, invites your reading. *Coaching Young Athletes* is a must for all those concerned about young people and sport in our country today!

Steve Combs
Executive Director
U.S. Wrestling Federation

Acknowledgment

The authors would like to acknowledge the collective efforts of hundreds of sports scientists from whom the information in this volume is based. We also wish to recognize the contribution of the Coaching Association of Canada who pioneered the development of a national coaching education program. And we wish to thank the thousands of coaches who taught us how to teach them!

About the Authors

Rainer Martens, director of the Office of Youth Sports and a professor of sport psychology at the University of Illinois, is a leader in the development of educational programs for youth coaches. He is a member of the National Council of Kid's Wrestling, the National Physical Fitness Board of the Boy's Clubs of America, and is the sports psychologist for the US Olympic Nordic Ski Team. Rainer is author of *Joy and Sadness in Children's Sports*

Rainer Martens, PhD

and co-editor of *Guidelines for Children's Sports*. He has conducted numerous coaching clinics in nearly every sport. A former wrestler and baseball player, Rainer now enjoys handball, and with his wife Marilyn, hiking and cross-country skiing.

Bob Christina is a professor of physical education and director of the Motor Behavior Research Laboratory at The Pennsylvania State University. A former high school

Bob Christina, PhD

and college athlete, Bob has extensive experience as a volunteer and professional coach in baseball, football, basketball, wrestling, and golf. In 1972 he was named the "Coach of the Year" in baseball in the New York Athletic Conference. He has conducted coaching clinics for the US Wrestling Federation, New York State Sports Authority, National Rifle Association, Little League Baseball, US Ski Coaches Association, and the US Field Hockey Association. Bob enjoys playing golf, racquetball, and jogging, and with his wife Barbara, hiking and tennis.

Jack Harvey, MD

Jack Harvey, founder and director of the Fort Collins Sports Medicine Clinic, received his MD degree at the University of Texas Medical School where he combined his keen interest in sports with medicine. Jack serves as sports medicine consultant to the US Wrestling Federation, US Olympic Nordic Ski Team, the Denver Broncos Football Club, and local high school teams. A member of the American College of Sports Medicine, he has contributed many sports medicine articles to national medical journals. Despite his busy schedule, Jack finds time to cycle, row, mountain climb, and ski with his wife O'Linda.

Brian Sharkey, PhD

Brian Sharkey is internationally reknowned for his development of award-winning fitness programs. He is the sport physiologist for the US Olympic Nordic Ski Team and a frequent consultant to US government agencies regarding fitness. His book, *Physiology of Fitness,* is used in hundreds of college fitness courses as well as by coaches to develop training programs for their athletes. Brian is a dedicated long distance runner and skilled backpacker. He and his wife Barbara enjoy tennis and cross-country skiing together.

The Coach

Meet the Coach. You will see a great deal of him and his friends throughout the book, so we thought you should get acquainted with him now. Our bulbous-nosed hero is basically an old time coach filled with emotion and "Lombardi-isms," who constantly comes up against the changing attitudes in the world of sports. But Coach shows that "old dogs can learn new tricks" as he changes his coaching behaviors to be consistent with the philosophy advocated in this book.

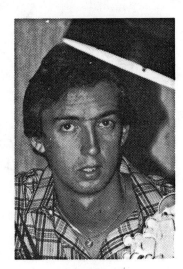

Paul Reynolds

Paul Reynolds is the illustrator and creator of the cartoon strip in which the Coach stars. Paul, who is 6 feet 8 inches tall and a former college and semi-pro basketball player, began his cartoon strip HEY COACH! as his basketball career ended. He relies on many of his own experiences as material for the activities of the Coach. Paul now resides in San Carlos, California where he pursues his career as an artist.

Becoming a Successful Coach

Welcome to coaching. If you've not coached before, you have many new experiences awaiting you. Perhaps you've already daydreamed scenes with the kids carrying you off the field on their shoulders after winning the championship and your friends and neighbors congratulating you for masterminding the perfect season. Or perhaps your daydreams turn to nightmares—you see yourself hitting infield practice before the game, but you keep missing the ball and the parents of the other team begin snickering. Then later in the game you make a tactical blunder and some loudmouth parent ridicules you in front of everyone.

Like any profession coaching has its highs and lows, but if you are prepared, it can be mostly highs. If you have the teaching skills of a wise educator, the medical knowledge of a physician, the administrative leadership of a business executive, and the counseling wisdom of a psychologist, you should throw this book away; it won't help you. But if you don't, join us to find out what makes a coach successful.

Is it winning games? Yes, in part, winning is one aspect of successful coaching. Coaches who teach skills effectively and who nourish the enthusiasm of youngsters are much more likely to win than coaches who don't. But a successful coach is much more than a winning coach. Successful coaches help young athletes to enjoy mastering new skills, to enjoy competing with others, and to feel good about themselves. Successful coaches not only are well-versed in the technique or skills of their sport, they know how to teach these skills to young people. And successful coaches not only teach children the skills of the sport, they also teach and model the skills needed for successful living in our society.

In short, being a successful coach is a challenge. And good intentions are not enough to be successful; you need all the knowledge you can get. That's why we have written *Coaching Young Athletes*. In this book, you will learn about the *science of coaching*. (Many books about technique and strategies are already available, and we've listed some of the better ones for many different sports in Appendix B).

In this introductory book you will learn about the following sport sciences:

Sport Psychology

Sport Pedagogy

Sport Physiology

Sports Medicine

Don't worry when you come across new terms such as *sport pedagogy*. We'll introduce these sport sciences to you in understandable and, we hope, entertaining ways. We don't want to frighten you away with a bunch of scientific mumbo-jumbo, but part of learning to be a more effective coach requires you to learn some new terms. Just as carpenters must know about miter boxes, soffits and wainscots, modern day coaches need to know about aerobic and anaerobic training, isokinetic exercises, heat stroke, sprains and strains, feedback, instructional goals, intrinsic motivation, and competitive anxiety. In this book you will find out about all these things and much more to help you become a better coach.

Most coaches used to learn the skills of coaching through years of trial and error. But oh, how some of those errors hurt! *Coaching Young Athletes* will help you shorten that learning process—and reduce those errors—by drawing upon the wisdom of experienced and knowledgeable coaches and the research of hundreds of sport scientists who have studied sport over the past 30 years.

This book, however, does not contain all the information you will need. We're not holding back, but as you probably suspect, we don't have all the answers! Although we have three PhDs and an MD to our collective credit, and even though we spend much of our time studying sport (and most of the rest playing sports), we still have much to learn. Thus, this book is only one source of information for you. Another way you can learn is to watch and talk with other coaches. They can teach you both effective and ineffective coaching practices; what you must do is distinguish between the two. *Coaching Young Athletes* will help you do that by providing you with a foundation in sports medicine and science.

It won't take too long to read *Coaching Young Athletes*, but it may take some time to *know* its contents, and perhaps even

longer to put into practice what you know. Just as a youngster doesn't learn to play shortstop overnight, you won't learn the skills of coaching in a day. You will need to read and reread parts of this book, observe other coaches and yourself, and practice the skills we describe. As you undertake this self-study, you will see that successful coaches are those who can learn new skills, who are flexible enough to change old ways when change is needed, who can accept constructive criticism, and who are able to critically evaluate themselves. Throughout *Coaching Young Athletes*, we will ask you to do all these things. In fact, we are going to urge you to put forth the same effort you will expect from the young athletes you coach.

Part 1

Developing A Coaching Philosophy

CHAPTER 1
Your Coaching Objectives

CHAPTER 2
Your Coaching Style

In Part 1, we ask you to think about the two most important decisions a coach makes. We discuss the first decision in chapter 1, in which we ask you to consider what objectives you will seek to attain as a coach. In chapter 2, we ask you to think about the coaching style you will use to attain them.

How you make these decisions will form your coaching philosophy and, to a large extent, determine how much success and enjoyment you and your athletes will have. Although we obviously cannot make these decisions for you, we will encourage you to make these decisions in a certain way.

CHAPTER 1

Your Coaching Objectives

One of the two most important decisions you will make as a coach concerns the objectives you seek. Most sports authorities recognize three major objectives:

1. To have a **winning** team;

2. To have **fun**—both you and your players;

3. To help young people **develop** . . .
   (a) physically, by learning sports skills, improving physical conditioning, developing good health habits, and avoiding injuries.
   (b) psychologically, by learning to control their emotions and to develop feelings of self-worth.
   (c) socially, by learning how to cooperate in a competitive context and by learning appropriate standards of behavior (sportsmanship).

Which of these objectives are important to you? Winning? Having fun? Helping kids develop? Perhaps you believe all three are important. But what if you must choose between them, which at times you will? Coaches often must decide whether they will pursue victory at the possible expense of the young athlete's well-being or development. What will be your priorities then?

Assessing Your Objectives

Below is a short questionnaire for you to complete which will help you to decide about your objectives for **winning,** having **fun**, and helping young athletes **develop**.

Read each statement and the three options which follow it. Decide which of the three you feel is most important and write "most" in the blank next to that option. Then decide which of the three options is least important to you and write "least" in the blank. Put a check (✔) mark in the blank for the item not chosen. Although in some cases you may think all three choices are important, indicate which is the *most* important and which is the *least* important of the three. Try to answer each question as you honestly feel.

Now let's score the test. Each item which you marked *most* is assigned a score of 3, each item marked *least* is scored a 1, and the item you checked (✔) but did not select is scored a 2. In the following chart, write in the numerical value for each item in the adjacent open square. Begin by scoring Question 1, item A. If you selected it as the *most*

Your Coaching Objectives

1. The best coaches are those who:
   ____ A. Give individual help and are interested in young athletes' development.
   ____ B. Make practices and games fun.
   ____ C. Teach athletes the skills needed to win.
2. If a story was written about me in the newspaper, I would like to be described as:
   ____ D. A winning coach.
   ____ E. A coach who contributed to the development of young people.
   ____ F. A coach for whom athletes enjoyed playing.
3. As a coach I emphasize:
   ____ G. Having fun.
   ____ H. Winning.
   ____ I. Teaching skills that young people can use later in life.

Score Your Objectives

		Development	Fun	Winning
Question 1	A			
	B			
	C			
Question 2	D			
	E			
	F			
Question 3	G			
	H			
	I			
TOTAL				

important you will write a 3 in the open square, if you selected it as the *least* important you will write a 1, and if you checked (✔) it you will write a 2. Do the same now for B through I.

Now add up the scores in each column. Each of your totals should range somewhere between 3 and 9, the higher your total the more you emphasize that outcome. The first column shows your priority for the **development** of young athletes, the second column your priority for having **fun**, and the third column the ranking you gave **winning**.

Most coaches' scores indicate winning is least important, and development of young athletes is most important. Did you answer the same way? Is it true of how you coach?

A Philosophy of Winning—A Winning Philosophy

No single decision is more important in determining how you coach than your priority about these objectives—especially the significance you give to winning. Some coaches who say winning is least important don't behave that way when they coach. For example, when coaches play only their best athletes, when they play injured athletes, or when they scream disparaging remarks at athletes who have erred, they obviously believe winning is more important than athletes' development.

Be honest. Do you at times overemphasize winning? Do you at times make decisions that reflect more concern about winning the game than the development of the athletes? It is easy to do in a society that places so much value on winning!

We have a philosophy about winning that we want you to consider. It is a philosophy that experienced and successful youth coaches, professional educators, and physicians all endorse. It is a philosophy we hope you will endorse, and more importantly, one you will put into practice! Our philosophy is simple:

ATHLETES FIRST
WINNING SECOND

What we mean by this is also quite simple: Every decision you make and every behavior you display is based first on what you think is best for your athletes, and second, on what may improve the athlete's or team's chances of winning. It is the philosophical foundation for the Bill of Rights for Young Athletes which is presented on page 7. We hope you do more than just read these Rights. Think about how you can help ensure that each athlete keeps them.

We all know that winning is out of perspective in some youth sports programs, something which critics frequently like to point out. Some critics, in fact, are urging that competitive sports programs be eliminated entirely and replaced with coopera-

petition. To play sports without striving to win is to be a "dishonest competitor," says Michael Novak in *Joy of Sports*.

"Winning isn't everything, it's the only thing," said Vince Lombardi, or so we are told. Actually Lombardi did not say it quite that way; that was a reporter's mutation. What Lombardi actually said was, "Winning isn't everying, but striving to win is." And that statement more accurately reflects his coaching philosophy.

Does it make sense that the emphasis on winning should not be on the winning itself, but the striving to win? It's the pursuit of the victory, the dreams of achieving the goal more than the goal itself that yields the joy of sports. Many outstanding athletes candidly say that their best memories of sport are not of the victories themselves, but the months of preparation, anticipation, and the self-revelation before and during the competition.

Commitment

Competition, and the striving to win, are significant in another way. Today we hear much about our alienated youth, their lack of commitment to our established institutions, and their lack of desire to achieve excellence. Sadly, many young people are not finding activities in their home, school, or place of worship worthy of their commitment. But America's youth are being "turned on" by sports; they find sports a challenge worth pursuing. And what is that challenge? It is the competition—the comparison of abilities and efforts, the striving to win, and the recognition for excellence achieved.

Larry Smith was one of these "uncommitted" youth; he was too lazy or disinterested to do his school work, he usually sat around the house watching television and eating, which resulted in his becoming overweight. But for some unknown reason Larry went

tive games. They argue that competition creates hostility and is unproductive, whereas cooperation builds friendship and produces the greatest achievements of man. We disagree with their evaluation of competition. Eliminating competition will not put winning in proper perspective; that's "throwing out the baby with the bath water." Competition is neither good nor evil as such—it is merely a means by which we compare our abilities and efforts with others under some agreed-upon rules. Whether competition is healthy depends upon *how* we compete and what significance we place on winning.

Striving to Win

We are not suggesting that winning is unimportant. Winning, or more accurately, *striving to win*, is essential to enjoyable com-

BILL OF RIGHTS FOR YOUNG ATHLETES

Right to participate in sports

Right to participate at a level commensurate with each child's maturity and ability

Right to have qualified adult leadership

Right to play as a child and not as an adult

Right of children to share in the leadership and decision-making of their sport participation

Right to participate in safe and healthy environments

Right to proper preparation for participation in sports

Right to an equal opportunity to strive for success

Right to be treated with dignity

Right to have fun in sports

out for football, where at last he found a challenge. To make the team and meet the maximum weight limit, he needed to improve his grades and lose 10 pounds. His parents and teachers had tried to get him to do both for months, but had failed. Now he did them on his own accord!

Recently, a 16-year-old mentally retarded boy received an award on national television for his outstanding accomplishment as a swimmer. What was remarkable about this young man was that at the age of 12 he could not speak or perform the basic self-help skills of feeding and dressing. But through the Special Olympics, he learned to swim and to compete—and this challenge brought him out of his inner world. He not only learned to feed and dress himself, he learned to speak and, even more remarkably, to teach other young people how to swim.

In discussing some of our schools' problems, the noted educator James Coleman observed that man's great accomplishments

come about when individuals make an intense commitment to something; when only a total concentrated effort may result in success—but even then success is not guaranteed. Sports attract that type of commitment and often result in great personal accomplishment.

Sportsmanship

The element of *competition* in sports has value in another way. Through sport young people can develop morally—to learn a basic code of sportsmanship that transfers to a moral code of life. Competitive sports—where winning is a valued prize—provides opportunities for higher levels of moral development to occur.

For example, Sharon is playing a recreational game of tennis with Susan, who hits the winning point on the baseline. Knowing that the shot was good, Sharon so declares it. Susan wins. Now that's not so hard to do when you're playing tennis only for fun, when there is little or nothing at stake.

But now Sharon is playing the same game and winning means a trip to Hawaii, a cash prize of $100, and the prestigious city championship. It takes a great deal more to make the proper call in this situation.

One value of competitive sports is that situations which require such moral decisions occur *often*, and they provide youngsters with the opportunity to learn and adults the opportunity to model appropriate sportsmanship. To make the appropriate moral judgment at the expense of a valued victory is a real test of character as well as an opportunity to build character.

Keeping Winning in Perspective

Winning is important in sports. And winning can be kept in perspective when adults recognize that the process of striving to win can bring out the best in young people—in their performance, commitment, and moral development. For sports to provide these benefits, it is vital that you maintain a proper perspective about winning: **Athletes First, Winning Second.** Will you be able to keep winning in perspective not only now but during the heat of a contest, not only when you are winning but when you are losing, not only when things go right but when things go wrong?

When winning is kept in perspective, sports programs produce children who enjoy movement, who strive for excellence, who dare to risk error to learn, and who grow with both praise and constructive criticism. When winning is kept in perspective, there is room for fun in the pursuit of victory, or more accurately, the pursuit of victory *is* fun. With proper leadership, sports programs produce children who accept responsibilities, who accept others and, most of all, who accept themselves.

CHAPTER 2

Your Coaching Style

The second important decision you need to make is about your coaching style. Your coaching style will determine how you decide what skills and strategies you will teach, how you will organize for practice and competition, what methods you will use to discipline players, and most importantly, what role you will permit the athletes to have in making decisions.

Three Coaching Styles

Most coaches lean toward one of three coaching styles: the command style, the submissive style, or the cooperative style.

Command Style

With this style, the coach makes all the decisions. The role of the athlete is to respond to the coach's commands. The assumption underlying this approach is that the coach has knowledge and experience, and thus, it is his or her role to tell the athlete what to do. The athlete's role is to listen, to absorb, and to comply.

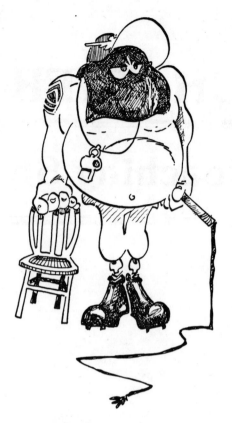

Submissive Style

Coaches who adopt this style make as few decisions as possible. It's a throw-out-

the-ball-and-have-a-good-time approach. The coach provides almost no instructions, exerts as little influence on the athletes as possible, and resolves discipline problems only when absolutely necessary. Coaches who adopt this style either lack the competence to provide instruction and guidance, are too lazy to meet the demands of their coaching responsibilities, or are very misinformed about what coaching is. The submissive style coach is merely a babysitter—and often a poor one at that. We urge you not to adopt this style.

Cooperative Style

Coaches who select the cooperative style share with athletes the making of decisions. Although they recognize their responsibility to provide leadership and guide children toward achieving the objectives set forth, cooperative style coaches also recognize that youngsters cannot become responsible adults without having the opportunity to share in the decision-making.

Coaching Styles Evaluated

Which style best describes you: command, submissive, or cooperative? The command style has been prevalent in the past and is a highly visible style among many professional, college, and high school coaches. Novice or inexperienced coaches often adopt the command style because it was the style used by a former coach or the style of a coach whom they have seen or about whom they have read. Sometimes coaches adopt this style because it helps them conceal their own doubts about their capabilities. If they don't permit the athletes to question them, if they can avoid explaining why they coach as they do, then their inadequacies won't be uncovered—or so they think!

Although the command style was readily accepted by athletes in the past, it is poorly received by young athletes today and is seldom successful. Moreover, you may find that this style forces you to be the type of coach you do not want to be because it is incompatible with your objectives.

On the surface the command style appears effective. Good athletic teams need organization. They cannot be effectively run as participant democracies; you cannot have the team take a vote on every decision that needs to be made. The command style is effective if winning is the primary objective and as long as its authoritarian nature does not stifle athletes' motivation. Indeed, this is one of the major limitations of the command style. Rather than athletes playing because they are intrinsically motivated, they play for the praise of the coach or to avoid his or her wrath.

The command style is increasingly being rejected today, not only by coaches of younger athletes, but by coaches of adult athletes, for it treats athletes as robots or slaves, not as thinking human beings. Coaches are recognizing that the command style alienates all but the highly gifted and

diminishes their own satisfaction in relating to athletes.

Coaches who use the command style prevent athletes from fully enjoying the sport. The accomplishments are the coaches', not the athletes'.

The command style is not compatible with our philosophy: **Athletes First, Winning Second.** If your objective is to help young people grow physically, psychologically, and socially through sport; if your objective is to increase the athlete's capacity for making decisions; if your objective is to help young people become independent, then the command style is not for you.

We obviously favor the cooperative style, because it shares the decision-making with the athletes and is compatible with our philosophy. Some people think the cooperative style means you abandon your responsibilities as coach or that you let athletes do anything they want. That's not the case at all!

Cooperative style coaches provide athletes with the structure and rules that make it possible for athletes to develop the capacity to set their own goals and to learn to strive for them. Being a cooperative style coach does not mean you avoid rules and order;

to not structure the activities of the team is to neglect a major responsibility of being a coach. The coach is faced with the complex task of deciding how much structure provides an optimum climate for the development of the athlete. The cooperative style is like handling a wet bar of soap—if you hold it too tight, it will squirt out of your hands (command style). If you don't grasp it firmly enough, it will slip away (submissive style). Firm but gentle pressure is what is needed. The cooperative style coach gives direction and provides instruction when it is needed, but also knows when it is useful to let athletes make decisions and assume responsibility.

> The cooperative style coach gives direction and provides instruction when it is needed.

We know there is more to being an athlete than just having certain motor skills. Athletes must be able to cope with pressures, adapt to changing situations, keep the game in perspective, exhibit discipline, and maintain concentration in order to perform well. These ingredients are nurtured by cooperative style coaches, but seldom by command style coaches. The cooperative style places more trust in the athlete, which has a positive effect on his or her self-image. It changes the social-emotional climate to one of greater openness. The cooperative style improves communication and also motivation. Athletes are motivated not out of fear of the coach, but for their personal satisfaction. Thus, the cooperative style is almost always more fun for athletes.

The cooperative style, however, has some drawbacks. This style requires more skill on the part of the coach. It means that

coaches must be in control of themselves. It means that every situation seldom has an absolute right or wrong answer. It means that coaches must individualize their coaching much more than when using the command style. Finally, it means that the coach may at times have to sacrifice winning in the interest of the athlete's well-being. When we discuss sport psychology and sport pedagogy, we will show you how to use the cooperative style.

What Makes A Successful Coach?

Earlier, we said successful coaches must have a good knowledge of the sport sciences. We also stated that successful coaches have their program objectives in the right priority. In this chapter, we suggest that successful coaches adopt a coaching style that is compatible with those objectives. And we tried not to be vague about what we thought were the right priorities! In this final section, we briefly describe three other attributes of successful coaches which we have thus far only indirectly mentioned:

- Knowledge of the sport
- Motivation to be a good coach
- Empathy

Knowledge of the Sport

There is no substitute for knowing well the techniques, rules, and strategies of the sport you coach. Sometimes we believe it is less important to have this knowledge when teaching beginning compared with advanced athletes, but this assumption is false. In fact, teaching the fundamentals well to beginning athletes requires as much knowledge, if not more, as coaching professional athletes. (Actually they require different types of knowledge.)

A lack of knowledge in teaching skills risks injury and frustration from repeated failure. The more knowledge you have of the basic skills of a sport, and the more you know about teaching these basics in the proper sequence, the more fun you and your athletes will have.

Moreover, your ability to teach these skills will earn you a great deal of respect from the youngsters, for they place high value on them. This respect gives you credibility, which you can use in teaching young athletes other important things, such as sportsmanship, emotional control, respect for others, and respect for themselves.

Having once played the sport is, of course, the most common way coaches acquire knowledge about techniques, rules, and strategies. But sometimes having played the sport doesn't give you all the knowledge you need, nor does not having played it mean you can't acquire this knowledge. Most communities have sources of information about the sport you coach. Technique clinics are frequently offered in most larger communities. Check with your school coach or community youth sport administrator to learn about the availability of these clinics. Many books are available for most sports (some of the better ones are listed in Appendix B). You can learn, too, by watching other coaches in your league as well as those at the high school and college level. Just remember, methods that may be appropriate with older athletes may not be appropriate for 10-year-olds.

Motivation

You can have all the skills and knowledge in the world, but without the motivation to want to use them, you will not be a successful coach. Indeed, when you come across the youngster who has the ability but not the motivation to develop into an excellent athlete, you will know full well the importance of motivation.

Sometimes coaches have the motivation but they don't have the time. Or stated another way, they don't have sufficient motivation to make the time for doing the things necessary to be a successful coach. We hope you have the motivation; young people need the time.

Empathy

What is it? The ability to readily understand the thoughts, feelings, and emotions of your athletes and convey this to them. Successful coaches possess empathy. They are able to understand athletes' emotions of joy, frustration, anxiety, and anger. Coaches who have empathy are able to listen to their athletes and express their understanding of what was said. Coaches who have empathy rarely belittle, chastise, or diminish the self-worth of their athletes because they know how it feels to experience the loss of self-worth. Coaches who have empathy more readily communicate respect for their athletes, and in turn, receive more respect. Empathy: you need it to be a successful coach!

What Kind of Coach Are You?

Below are 7 items which summarize the major issues we have considered in chapters 1 and 2. Evaluate yourself as a coach by circling the answer that best describes you.

1. My priority of objectives when coaching is in the best interest of my athletes.
   1. Seldom
   2. Usually
   3. Always

2. My usual coaching style is:
   1. Submissive
   2. Command
   3. Cooperative

3. My motivation to coach is:
   1. Low
   2. Moderate
   3. High

4. I am able to keep winning in perspective.
   1. Seldom
   2. Usually
   3. Always

5. My knowledge of the technique, rules, and strategies of the sport is:
   1. Weak
   2. Average
   3. Strong

6. My knowledge of the sport sciences (sport psychology, physiology, etc.) is:
   1. Weak
   2. Average
   3. Strong

7. My ability to convey empathy is:
   1. Weak
   2. Moderate
   3. Strong

Total _____

What Kind of Coach Are You: Score Yourself

Add up your score and evaluate yourself according to the following scale.

7 - 10 points: Warning! You are hazardous to the health of our children. Please reconsider your desire to coach or reread this chapter and determine if you can improve your score. If you choose to continue to coach, please read carefully the remainder of this book at least three times.

11 - 14 points: You are on the right track, but you can definitely improve by learning more. Read this book at least twice.

15 - 18 points: You are well on your way to being a successful coach but there is room for improvement. Determine where improvement is needed and read this book at least once.

19 - 21 points: You're what the kids need. Don't ever quit coaching! You might just read the remaining chapters to see if we made any mistakes!

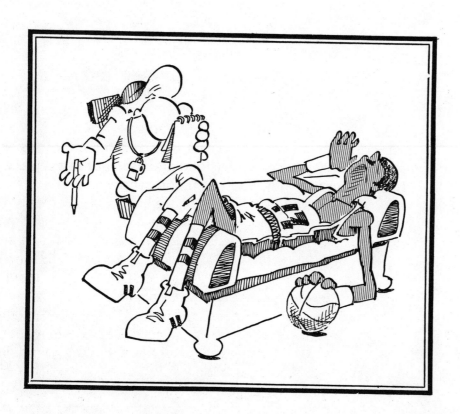

PART 2

Sport Psychology

CHAPTER 3
Evaluating Your
Communication Skills

CHAPTER 4
Developing Your
Communication Skills

CHAPTER 5
Principles of
Reinforcement

CHAPTER 6
Understanding
Motivation

Sport psychology is concerned with understanding why athletes and coaches behave as they do, sometimes in reaction to each other. It is a complex topic because human behavior is complex. Therefore you will want to read these next four chapters carefully, remembering that human behavior has few absolutes. These chapters offer recommendations as guidelines, not laws. They must be understood and used *not* as a replacement for, but in conjunction with, good common sense.

Over the past 15 years, sport psychologists have learned much that is of value to coaches, but only recently have coaches and athletes become aware of this knowledge. Today, sport psychologists are becoming an integral part of more and more professional, college, and Olympic sports programs because coaches and athletes alike are recognizing the importance of psychological factors in successful participation.

Although you'll want to learn about many aspects of sport psychology as you develop your coaching skills, none are more vital to coaching than learning how to communicate with young athletes and understanding what motivates them to play sports. In chapters 3 through 5, we will help you first evaluate and then develop your coaching communication skills, and in chapter 6, we will explain the complex factors influencing athletes' motivation.

CHAPTER 3

Evaluating Your Communication Skills

In this chapter, we discuss the fascinating subject of communication. Our purpose is to increase your awareness of the importance of communication in coaching and to permit you to evaluate your own communication skills.

Your success as a coach depends, to a large extent, on your ability to communicate effectively in countless situations, including:

- when parents speak to you about their child not playing enough,

- when you explain how to perform a complex skill,

- when your star player shows up late to the game and announces he or she is ready to play, or

- when you feel compelled to speak to the official who just made a call you are certain was incorrect.

Although coaches must be able to communicate with young people, fellow coaches, and parents equally well, to simplify our presentation, we will focus on the communication process between coach and athlete. All of the principles put forth, however, are equally applicable when adults communicate with each other.

Three Things You Need to Know About Communication

First, communication consists not only of sending messages, but also of receiving them. Although many coaches believe they are quite skilled at the former, they often are weak at the latter. Coaches need listening skills to not only hear but understand what is being said.

Second, communication consists of nonverbal messages as well as verbal messages. Gestures of hostility, facial expressions of joy, acts of intimidation, and behaviors of kindness are all forms of nonverbal communication. It has been estimated that over 70% of communication is nonverbal.

Third, as shown in Figure 3.1, communication is composed of two parts: content and emotion. Content refers to the *substance* of the message, whereas emotion is how you *feel* about it. Content is usually expressed verbally, emotion nonverbally. Pressure-packed competitive sports challenge coaches to be in control of the content and the emotions they communicate.

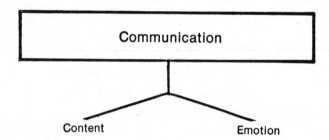

Figure 3.1—Components of communication.

How You Communicate

Communicating with your athletes consists of the following five steps:

1. You have thoughts (ideas, feelings, intentions) which you wish to convey.

2. You translate these thoughts into a message appropriate for transmission.

3. The message is transmitted through some channel (verbal or nonverbal).

4. The athlete receives the message (if he or she is paying attention) and interprets its meaning. The interpretation of the meaning of the message depends upon the athlete's comprehension of the message's content and your intentions.

5. The athlete responds internally to his or her interpretation of the message.

Sometimes this sequence of events flows smoothly, with you and the athlete clearly understanding the messages that both of you are sending. But sometimes problems occur within one or more of the five steps. Let's look at two examples.

Example 1

Coach: (shouting) "How many times do I have to tell you to use a cross-over step?"

Athlete: (meekly) "Sorry. I forgot."

Coach's intention: To give the athlete feedback about an error in technique and to encourage him to remember it in the future.

Athlete's interpretation: He thinks I'm lousy. I want to do it right, but there are so many things to remember. The harder I try the more nervous I get and the more mistakes I make. I wish he'd get off my back.

What went wrong in this communication? The coach's intent was good: to give constructive feedback. The method he chose to transmit the message, in both content and emotion, however, was not. The athlete received the message negatively, and instead of helping him to correct the error, it added to the pressure he felt.

The same message, however, expressed to another athlete may be interpreted to mean: "Darn, I did it wrong again. Coach is upset. I don't blame him. I ought to be getting it right and he's just trying to help."

In this case, even though the coach was not skillful in delivering the message, the athlete was able to understand the coach's intent and interpreted the message positively.

Example 2

Coach: "I thought you really played well today, John."

John: (with a tone of disbelief) "Uh huh. Thanks."

Coach's intention: To praise John for a good performance in hopes that he will do the same in the future.

John's interpretation: He's only saying that because we won. When we lose, even if I play well, he yells at me and the team.

The coach's thoughts were good and the message he intended to send was accurately transmitted. Unfortunately, the athlete's perception of the message's intent, not the content, was misinterpreted. This may have been the result of previous messages which led the athlete to believe that winning is more important to the coach than the players. Because the coach had lost credibility with John, a well-intended message was construed negatively.

Why Communications Are Ineffective

The reasons for ineffective communication between coach and athlete include any or all of the following:

1. The content of what you wish to communicate may be wrong for the situation.

2. The transmission of the message does not communicate what you intend it to because you lack the verbal or nonverbal skills needed to send the message.

3. The athlete doesn't receive the message because he or she isn't paying attention.

4. The athlete misinterprets the content of the message or fails to understand it, lacking the listening or nonverbal skills to interpret it.

5. The athlete understands the content, but misinterprets the intent of the message.

6. The messages sent are inconsistent over time, leaving the athlete confused about what is meant.

Clearly, ineffective communication is not always the fault of the coach; the problem may lie with the athlete, or with both coach and athlete. With the necessary communication skills, though, you can do much to avoid these problems. We will discuss these skills after we give you a chance to evaluate your communication skills.

Evaluating Your Communication Skills

From interviews and observations of hundreds of coaches, we have identified eight communication skills which coaches most need. We have described these eight skills, or rather, the *lack* of them through caricatures. Read the description of each coach and then rate yourself on the communication skills discussed. Circle the number which best describes you. If you have not coached before, answer according to how you communicate in a leadership position.

Pretentious Pete

Never admitting to an error, Pretentious Pete finds he doesn't get the respect he demands because he doesn't show any for his athletes. When he speaks, they tune out because what he says never amounts to much or is usually negative. Pretentious Pete has not yet learned that he cannot demand respect; it must be earned.

Do you have credibility with your athletes or are you like Pretentious Pete? Rate your credibility.

1	2	3	4	5
Very Low				Very High

Coach Badnews

Most of the words and actions of Coach Badnews are negative, sometimes almost hostile. She frequently criticizes her athletes, increasing their self-doubts and destroying their self-confidence. She is slow to praise, as if it is not "coach-like" to say a kind word. When an infrequent kindness is uttered, it is usually overshadowed by other negative comments.

Are you primarily positive in the messages you deliver or are you like Coach Badnews? Rate the degree to which your messages are positive or negative.

1	2	3	4	5
Negative				Positive

The Judge

The Judge constantly evaluates his athletes instead of giving them instructions. When players err, The Judge places blame rather than providing feedback or information about how to correct the error. When the players do well, The Judge cheers them on but doesn't know how to instruct them to achieve advanced levels of skill.

Do you give ample feedback and instructions or are you like The Judge? Rate the extent to which the content of your communication is high in information or high in judgment.

1	2	3	4	5
High in Judgment				High in Information

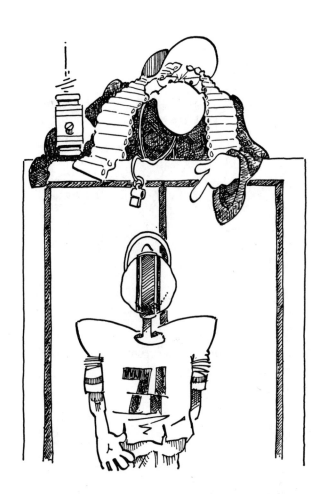

happens to be his star goalie. He tells the players not to argue with the officials, but then he constantly does so.

Are you consistent in your communication or are you like Coach Fred Fickle? Rate the consistency of your communication.

1	2	3	4	5
Inconsistent				Consistent

Coach Gabby

Coach Gabby is the most loquacious person you ever met. She constantly gives instructions in practice, and when not yelling advice to her players during the contest, she is muttering to herself on the sidelines. She is so busy talking that she never has time to listen to her athletes. It never occurred to her that her players might like to tell her something rather than always being told.

Fred Fickle

You are never sure what Coach Fred Fickle will say next. Today it's one thing, tomorrow it's another. Last week he punished Billy for fighting, but not Michael, who

Are you a good listener or are you like Coach Gabby? Rate how good a listener you are.

1	2	3	4	5
Not Good				Very Good

Old Stoneface

Old Stoneface never shows emotion. He doesn't smile, wink, or give his athletes a pat on the back. Nor does he scowl, kick at the dirt, or express disgust with them. You just don't know how he feels, which leaves some of the young players feeling insecure.

Are you able to communicate nonverbally or are you like Old Stoneface? Rate your nonverbal communication skills.

1	**2**	**3**	**4**	**5**
Weak				Strong

Professor Gobbledygook

The Professor just isn't able to explain anything at a level understandable to his players. Either he speaks to them as if they were fellow professors or so circuitously that the players are left confused. In addition, the Professor, who is used to dealing with abstractions, is unable to demonstrate the skills of the sport in a logical sequence so that the athletes can grasp the fundamentals.

Are you able to provide clear instructions and demonstrations or are you like Pro-

fessor Gobbledygook? Rate your ability to communicate instructions.

1	**2**	**3**	**4**	**5**
Weak				Strong

Coach Jellybean

Coach Jellybean just doesn't seem to understand how the principles of reinforcement work. Although he often gives jelly-

bean rewards to his athletes, he reinforces the wrong behavior at the wrong time. When faced with misbehavior, he either lets the misbehavior pass or comes down too hard on the athlete.

Do you understand the principles of reinforcement or are you like Coach Jellybean? Rate your skill in rewarding and punishing athletes.

1	2	3	4	5
Not Skilled				Highly Skilled

Coaches' Communication Awards

Now add up your eight ratings and write the total score here._____ Find which category your score falls into below and accept the award you deserve.

36-40 Golden Tongue Award. You are destined for success.

31-35 Silver Tongue Award. Good, but you can be better. Read on.

26-30 Bronze Tongue Award. O.K., but you have plenty of room for improvement. Read on *carefully*.

21-25 Leather Tongue Award. Given to those who frequently place their foot in their mouth.

8-20 The Muzzle Award. Until you improve, wear it. Read the next two chapters each night for a month.

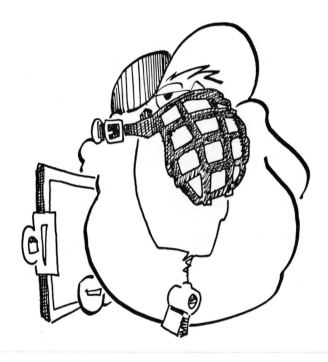

If you are not the recipient of the Golden Tongue Award, the next two chapters will help you develop the communication skills needed to earn it.

CHAPTER 4

Developing Your Communication Skills

In the last chapter you evaluated yourself on eight communication skills. In this chapter we focus on six of them, as follows:

- Developing credibility when you communicate.

- Communicating with a positive approach.

- Sending messages high in information.

- Communicating with consistency.

- Learning how to listen.

- Improving your nonverbal communication skills.

The seventh skill, applying the principles of reinforcement, is discussed in chapter 5 and the eighth, instructional communication skills, is examined in chapter 8.

Developing Credibility When You Communicate

Can you think of someone who has very little credibility with you—a fellow worker, a neighbor, a politician perhaps? Do you know a coach like Pretentious Pete? You don't put much stock in almost anything this person says. Why? It's probably for one of the following reasons:

1. You believe they are not knowledgeable about what they say.

2. Usually whatever they say makes little sense or is of no importance to you.

3. They often distort things or simply lie so that you have little trust in them.

4. They constantly speak negatively.

5. They speak to you as though you were stupid or less important than they.

Your credibility is probably the single most important element in communicating effectively with your athletes. Your communication credibility is reflected in your athletes' attitude about the trustworthiness of what you say. At the outset, youngsters will give you plenty of credibility because you occupy the prestigious role of the *coach*. From thereon, however, it is up to you whether you maintain and build this credibility or diminish it. You can build credibility by doing the following:

1. Being a cooperative style coach.

2. Being knowledgeable about the sport, or at least being honest about the knowledge you possess.

3. Being reliable, fair, and consistent in dealing with your athletes.

4. Expressing warmth, friendliness, acceptance, and empathy.

5. Being dynamic, spontaneous, and open.

6. Using the positive approach—the next communication skill.

Communicating With A Positive Approach

One of the most important skills you can learn, for coaching or any other aspect of life, is to communicate with a positive approach. The positive appproach emphasizes praise and rewards to strengthen desirable behaviors, whereas the negative approach uses punishment and criticism to eliminate undesirable behaviors. The positive approach helps athletes value themselves as individuals, and in turn it gives you credibility. The negative approach increases fear of failure, lowers self-esteem, and destroys your credibility.

The positive approach does not mean that every message should be full of praise and gushy compliments. Too much praise leaves youngsters doubting the sincerity of your message and reduces the value of your rewards. It also does not mean that you turn your back on athletes' misbehaviors. At times, athletes should be punished, but you can do so in positive ways (see chapter 5).

The positive approach is an attitude that you communicate both in your verbal and nonverbal messages. It is an attitude that communicates a desire to understand, an

acceptance of others, and an expectation of mutual respect. *It is the attitude of a co-operative style coach.*

Bad Habit

But why do so many coaches behave like Coach Badnews? One of the reasons is that they simply fall into the habit of telling youngsters only what they do wrong rather than what they do right. Is this true of you? Don't think only about the content of your messages, but about the emotion expressed as well.

Breaking habits is difficult, especially well-ingrained habits as the negative approach often is. If you are uncertain whether you use the positive or negative approach, or the degree to which you use them, ask a fellow coach or friend to observe you for a constructive evaluation. *Warning*: This takes courage and a very good friend.

If you know you are in the habit of using the negative approach, you need to do three things to change to the positive approach. First, you must want to. Second, you must practice the positive approach not only when coaching but in all your communications. It's often most difficult to use the positive approach with those to whom you are closest, so if you're married, practice with your spouse. (Who knows, learning to

be a coach may help your marriage.) And third, you need to monitor yourself or get help from someone whom you will permit to tell you when your bad habit rears its ugly head.

Unrealistic Expectancies

Another reason coaches use the negative approach is that they have unrealistic expectancies about acceptable and unacceptable behaviors. Sometimes coaches forget that 8-year-olds are not 18-year-olds, or that one 14-year-old is not as skilled as another 14-year-old. When coaches have unrealistic expectations, they seldom view their athletes as successful. If coaches communicate to athletes their judgment of failure—and sometimes they do—athletes will feel frustrated and unaccepted.

It is equally important for coaches to not only have realistic goals about the athletes' performance capabilities, but also about their emotional and social behavior. Remember, it's natural for kids to "horse around" and have fun.

Being realistic in your expectations and recognizing the fallability of human behavior will make it much easier for you to be Coach Goodnews rather than Coach Badnews. Anyway remember: If young athletes behaved perfectly they wouldn't need you as a coach!

Short-term Success

The third reason coaches use the negative approach is that they honestly believe it gets the best results. This may be because so many college and professional coaches are seen using this approach.

The negative approach does work. It can help athletes learn the skills you want them to learn; it can motivate them to achieve. But when the criticism is frequent or continuous, the strong negative emotion it

YOU STINK JONES! WHEN ARE YOU GOING TO LEARN! NEXT TIME YOU SCREW UP IT'S 10 LAPS AROUND THE GYM!

creates in athletes often interferes with learning and motivation. Athletes will start playing it safe, taking as few risks as possible to avoid the coach's wrath. The negative approach is effective only for a short time; after awhile athletes "turn off" and the coach loses credibility.

Sending Messages High In Information

Some coaches seem to think that a whistle, cap, and the title "Coach" qualify them as The Judge. They constantly give verdicts to their players, telling them whether they did something right or wrong—usually wrong. But it's not enough to tell young athletes that they did something wrong; they need specific information about *how* to do it right. Successful coaches are not judges; they are skilled teachers.

Some coaches communicate like The Judge for the same reasons they adopt the negative approach—sheer habit and imita-

tion of other coaches who engage in this practice. Other coaches become judges because they lack the technical knowledge of the sport necessary for providing youngsters the information they need. When this occurs, coaches become judges to cover up for their own deficiencies. Command-style coaches are especially likely to communicate like The Judge.

Being a judge is dangerous; it assumes you always know what is good and bad, right and wrong. Too often coaches find themselves labeling something as bad or wrong, only to learn later that they were wrong.

Let's take an example: A boy is late to practice, so the coach makes him run 15 laps as punishment without giving him an opportunity to explain. Later, when the player gets a chance, he explains that his mother had not returned home and he was responsible for babysitting his little sister. Under these circumstances, the athlete behaved responsibly.

Consider another example: After a girl strikes out by swinging at a ball a foot over her head, the coach yells: "For Pete's sake! What's wrong with you? Don't you know a ball from a strike?" This message is highly destructive and provides no useful information to the athlete.

Remember, sports tend to evaluate enough through competition. A youngster knows when he or she has played poorly. Who needs to be told you made an error when the ball goes between your legs and the game-winning run scores. Athletes need some room to make mistakes—that's part of learning.

Provide evaluation when it's clear that athletes don't know what is correct or incorrect. If the behavior is good, praise them for it and tell them what is good about it. And if it's wrong, give them specific instructions on how they can improve.

The last season legendary coach John Wooden coached the UCLA basketball team, two psychologists recorded all of his verbal communications with his team during practice. Nearly 75% of Wooden's messages gave specific instructions to the athletes. His remaining messages consisted of 12% requests to hustle, 7% praise, and 6% scolds.

In another study, it was found that little league baseball coaches who provided more instructions were evaluated more positively by the players than were coaches who gave general encouragement. This was especially true for players who were low in self-esteem. Youngsters so dearly want to learn sports skills that not only will they respect you for helping them learn, they will respect themselves for having done so.

Habitually communicating in evaluative language also tends to make people feel uneasy around you. They become cautious, almost defensive; they always are wondering how you are evaluating them at the moment.

Although there is a time to communicate your evaluations, it should not dominate your communication with athletes. Save it for instructional sessions when you can put the evaluation into a constructive framework.

One final caution: Do not evaluate the athletes' selves. Instead, evaluate their behavior. Rather than saying to a youngster who has made a tactical error, "What's wrong with you, Joe?" it is better to say, "That was the wrong decision, Joe," commenting only on the behavior.

" THANKS FOR TEACHING ME HOW TO HEAD THE BALL COACH... IT'S EASY! "

Communicating With Consistency

Communicating with consistency when coaching is a real challenge, for each of us has a little Fred Fickle in us. It is so easy to preach one thing and do another, or to do one thing one day and then the opposite the next. Or sometimes your brain tells you to say one thing verbally, but your emotions express something else nonverbally. When youngsters receive these mixed messages, they become confused.

Look at it from the perspective of young athletes. A coach asks them to show emotional control when playing, but then throws a temper tantrum at an official. A coach asks

them to respect their teammates, but treats them disrespectfully. A coach tells them physical fitness is important, but does nothing to keep him or herself fit. A coach tells them to be self-confident, then turns around and destroys their feelings of self-worth by yelling at them for making an error. When coaches behave in this way, it is no wonder that youngsters think they are hypocrites!

Failing to keep your word is another form of inconsistency that can have devastating results. For example, you may promise the kids a reward if they have a good practice and then fail to deliver the reward. A few such occurrences and athletes learn not to trust you, which lessens your control over

---

Failing to keep your word can have devastating results.

---

them. If you don't deliver a promised reward, you in effect lose part of your reward power and may be forced to resort to punishment as a means of control.

Young athletes, however, are not out looking for inconsistencies in the coach. Because of the great respect they have for the title "coach" and for those who hold it, young athletes begin with the attitude that the coach can do no wrong, and thus will be slow to see inconsistencies. Because of this deep trust, when they do recognize a coach as a hypocrite or a liar, it can be a shattering experience to them.

Of course, coaches do not usually intend to be inconsistent or hypocritical; it is due more to carelessness in their behavior. It is so easy for coaches like Fred Fickle to forget the influence they have on the young athletes under their charge. Thus, it is so important to remember this: *Be as good as your word*. If you want your communications to positively control and influence your athletes, then you must be consistent.

Learning How To Listen

Are you a good listener? How much of what is said do you actually hear? If you are like most untrained listeners, it's probably between 15 and 20%.

Although listening seems easy, it is deceptively difficult. Coaches are often poor listeners because: (a) they are so busy "commanding" that they never give others a chance to speak, and (b) they assume that they know it all and that their young athletes have nothing to say which needs to be heard. "Children are to be seen, not heard," seems to be their attitude.

Poor listening skills cause a breakdown in the communication process. After repeated failures to get you to listen, athletes will simply quit speaking to you, and in turn, are less likely to listen to you. Also, coaches who are poor listeners often find they have more discipline problems. Youngsters sometimes will misbehave to get your attention—it's a drastic way to get the coach to listen.

Improving Your Listening Skills

You can do a number of things to improve your listening skills.

1. The most important, of course, is to recognize the need to listen.

2. Concentrate on listening. This means you must give your undivided attention to what is being said. Have you ever had someone accuse you of not listening? Although you may have heard the words and could repeat them, you were really not listening. What the accuser sensed was that you were not "with them" psychologically.

3. When listening, search for the meaning of the message rather than focusing on the details. Especially when in a disagreement, we are inclined to listen for and respond to details which we can attack or refute, failing to listen to the major point of the message.

4. Avoid interrupting your athletes. We sometimes interrupt others because we anticipate what they will say, so we complete their thought for them. Then we respond to what we thought they were going to say, perhaps later to discover that was not at all what they had intended to say. We also interrupt others especially if they speak slowly, because we lack the patience to hear them complete the message. Remember that you can listen considerably faster than a person can speak.

5. Respect the rights of your athletes to share their views with you. It is important not only to listen to their fears and problems, but to their joys and accomplishments. Your response to youngsters' views is important in shaping their attitudes.

6. Repress the tendency to respond emotionally to what is said (but don't be like Old Stoneface). Try to think why the athlete said what he or she did and how you can respond constructively. (We know this is easier said than done, but isn't this true of most complex skills?)

7. Ask questions when you do not understand something. The effective use of questions is an important part of what is called "active listening."

Active Listening

Educators have distinguished between two types of listening called "passive" and "active." Passive listening is what we usually think of as listening—being silent while the other person speaks. Although passive listening is sometimes desirable, it has limitations in that the speaker is not sure whether you are paying attention or whether you really understand what he or she is saying. Although listening communicates some degree of acceptance, athletes may think the coach is evaluating them. Silence does not communicate empathy and warmth.

Active listening, as opposed to passive listening (silence), involves interacting with athletes by providing them with proof that you understand. The following are some examples of how it works:

Before an important game, one of your players is worried about meeting your expectations.

Player: "Do you think we can beat this team?"

Coach: "They are a pretty good team, but we have a good team too."

Player: "But what if we don't play well?"

Now you must interpret these questions. Is she really worried about the team winning, or is she worried that she may not be able to play well enough herself? Active listening involves not guessing at your player's meaning but finding out. You find out by *feeding back* to the player what you think she means.

Coach: "Are you worried how you might play?"

Player: "Well, a little."

Coach: "As long as you try to do the best you can I'll always be proud of how you play."

The coach's reassurance lets the player know that her acceptance on the team is not contingent on her performing well, but only on her trying. Here is another example:

Gymnast: "What's the worst injury you've seen on the high bar?"

Coach: "I saw a fellow fly off and break his neck."

The coach may have answered the question without realizing what was really being asked. The player may have been expressing concern about his own possibility of being injured. Active listening by the coach might change the conversation this way.

Gymnast: "What's the worst injury you've seen on the high bar?"

Coach: "I've not seen too many injuries. Are you worried about getting hurt?"

Gymnast: "Sometimes I think about it."

Coach: "With the better equipment today and the use of a spotter, the chance of serious injury is really small."

Active listening is a tremendous skill which brings together many of the ideas we have discussed in this chapter. Active listening, however, works only when you convey that you accept your athletes' feelings and that you want to understand and help. Otherwise, you will come across as insincere, patronizing, or manipulative. Because active listening lets athletes know their ideas and feelings are respected and understood, they will be more willing to listen to you.

Improving Your Nonverbal Communication

If you ever needed to communicate with someone who does not speak the same language, you not only know how important nonverbal communication can be, but also how effective it can be. It is estimated that 70% of our total communication is nonverbal. In the world of sports, numerous situations arise in which effective nonverbal communication is essential to good performance, especially in team sports. Skilled nonverbal communication is equally important to you in your role as a coach.

Categories of Nonverbal Communication

Nonverbal communication, or what sometimes is called body language, falls into five different categories.

1. Body motion: includes gestures, movements of the hands, head, feet, and entire body. A tilt of the head, a furrow of the brow, or a shift of the eyes can communicate a great deal in the context of an ongoing interaction with another person.

2. Physical characteristics: includes physique, attractiveness, height, weight, body odors, and the like. Your own physical condition, for example, communicates the importance you give to physical fitness—not only when young, but throughout adulthood.

3. Touching behavior: includes pats on the back, taking someone by the hand, putting your arm around a player's shoulders, and so forth.

4. Voice characteristics: includes voice quality—its pitch, rhythm, resonance, inflections, etc. It often is not *what* we say, but *how* we say it that conveys the real message. For example, the comment, "You played a nice game today, Bill," can be said sincerely, with looks of approval, and voice qualities that indicate you truly mean it. Or it can be spoken sarcastically, with a slight

snarl on the face, indicating you mean exactly the opposite.

5. Body position: refers to the personal space between you and others and the position of your body with respect to theirs. The "cold shoulder" is an example of communication through body position. It refers to positions which tell you someone does not want to talk with you.

Are you aware of each of these dimensions of nonverbal communication, and are you effective in both sending and receiving nonverbal messages through each of these methods? Probably what skills you have in nonverbal communication were derived from on-the-job training the job of daily living. Teaching nonverbal communication skills by written or spoken words alone or learning nonverbal skills without practicing them is not easy.

Thus, your first step is to recognize the importance of nonverbal communication as part of the total communication process. One source for developing nonverbal skills is observing the feedback others give you as you both send and receive nonverbal messages. The value of the feedback depends on your sensitivity and receptivity to it. The more sensitive you become to nonverbal cues, the more likely you are to be able to express your feelings and attitudes nonverbally and to understand the athletes' feelings and attitudes. This is an important aspect of developing empathy which we discussed in chapter 2.

You as a Model

Once again, keep in mind that your every action on and off the playing surface is a form of nonverbal communication. We repeatedly emphasize this point because coaches seem to forget quickly that all their behaviors communicate, not just their good behaviors.

Perhaps one of the most important things you communicate by your actions is respect, or lack of it, for people and the sport. How you walk, how you approach others, your

gestures, and not only what you say but how you say it, all convey your attitudes about sportsmanship and other people. Young, impressionable athletes who hold you in high esteem are deeply impressed by everything you do.

Through your actions you can teach them a great deal more than the skills and rules of the sport. Lead the way in congratulating the opposing team after both victories and losses. Show them how you want them to behave in response to having played well or poorly, to having won or lost. Show them how they should handle situations when you think the team has been treated unfairly.

Young people, we find, are more influenced by what you do than by what you say. As the axiom states, "Actions speak louder than words." So if you want your athletes to display good sportsmanship, it is not enough to just tell them—you must show them!

The YMCA House Rules say it well:

Speak for yourself
Not for anybody else.

Listen to others
Then they'll listen to you.

Avoid put-downs
Who needs 'em?

Take charge of yourself
You are responsible for you.

Show respect
Every person is important.

Key Points to Remember

1. Having credibility with your athletes is essential for effective communication.

2. You can establish and maintain your credibility by being a cooperative style coach, being knowledgeable about the sport, being fair and consistent, being friendly and dynamic, and by using the positive approach.

3. By using the positive approach, you place emphasis on praise and rewards to strengthen desirable behaviors rather than using punishment to eliminate undesirable behaviors.

4. You can be more helpful to your athletes and maintain a better relationship with them by not judging them constantly. Instead provide athletes with specific instructions on how to perform the skill.

5. You can avoid destroying your credibility and confusing your athletes by being as consistent as possible in your communication.

6. You can improve your listening skills by not always talking and by recognizing that what your athletes have to say is important.

7. When you communicate to athletes that you heard and understood what they

said, you are using active listening skills.

8. Being skilled in such nonverbal communication as body motion and position, touching behaviors, and voice characteristics is highly important in your role as a coach.

9. Every action you make becomes a potentially important nonverbal message because your athletes see you as an example of how to behave.

CHAPTER 5

Principles of Reinforcement

You may have heard about behavior modification, a term which refers to the systematic use of the *Principles of Reinforcement*. Reinforcements refer to the consequences arising from our behavior. When we play golf well and get a low score, the consequence is that our playing partner has to buy dinner. When we don't play so well, we have to buy. When the consequence of doing something is positive—a *positive reinforcement*—we tend to do it again. When the consequence is negative—a *negative reinforcement*—we tend not to do it again. This is the first principle of reinforcement.

This and other principles of reinforcement can be a valuable part of your communication skills if applied correctly. Although the principles themselves are easy to understand, our credibility would suffer if we told you they were easy to apply with young athletes. They are simple to use with pigeons and rats, with whom these principles were first developed, but humans don't behave like pigeons or rats (not most of the time anyway).

Why are the principles of reinforcement more complex to use with humans? One reason is that each of us does not always react to positive and negative reinforcements in the same way. For example, having to sit on the bench for swearing may be punishment for one player, but it may provide another with the recognition he or she seeks from teammates.

Also positive- and negative-reinforced behavior cannot always be repeated at will if the athlete does not possess the skill to do so. For example, to be praised for hitting a homerun may instill a desire to hit more homeruns, but this does not mean the player has the skill to repeatedly do so. (In fact, the youngster may begin swinging for the fence too often, seeking more positive reinforcement, which has a negative effect on his or her overall hitting.)

A third reason the principles of reinforcement are complex is that you must consider all the reinforcements available as well as how someone values them in order to understand how he or she will behave. For example, even though your spouse yells at you for spending too much time coaching your team, this negative reinforcement may be far less than the positive reinforcement you get from coaching the team, so you keep coaching.

We want to impress upon you that the principles of reinforcement are complex because some psychologists have sold behavior modification as a "quick fix." This is untrue! Yet your understanding and application of what is known about behavior modification can be a valuable part of your communication skills. In the remainder of this chapter, we present the more important principles of reinforcement which are especially relevant for coaches.

Using Rewards

What Should You Reward?

Reward the performance not the outcome. When a boy hits a line drive to the shortstop who makes a great diving catch, the performance is good (line drive) the outcome is not (an out). When another player hits an easy fly ball to the left fielder who loses the ball in the sun and the batter ends up with a double, the performance was weak (easy flyball), but the outcome was good (a double). Rewarding the double reinforces luck not skill, and not rewarding

DON'T WORRY ABOUT LOSING THE RACE MELANIE! IT WAS YOUR BEST TIME EVER!

the line drive may cause the player to change his hitting method in search of a more favorable outcome.

Although coaches may know they should reinforce the performance and not the outcome, in the thick of competition this principle is often forgotten. We begin to think about winning and losing, not about how athletes are playing.

Reward athletes more for their effort than for their actual successes. When young athletes know you recognize they are trying to hit the ball, make the tackle, or run as fast as possible, they do not fear trying. If young athletes know you only reward them when they succeed, then they may begin to fear the consequences of failing. This causes anxiety in some youngsters.

Reward the little things along the way toward reaching a larger goal. If you wait to reward only the achievement of a major goal, you may never reward a youngster.

Reward not only the learning and performance of sports skills, but also the learning and performance of emotional and social skills. Reward your athletes for showing self-control, good judgment, and the ability to handle responsibility. (But you have to give them the responsibility first.) Reward them too for displaying good sportsmanship, teamwork, and cooperativeness.

How Often Should You Reward?

Reward frequently when a youngster is first learning a new skill. Generally, the greater the frequency, the faster the learning. One caution, though: If rewards are given insincerely or too freely, they lose their value.

Once the skill is well-learned, you only need to reinforce the behavior occasionally. Be careful, though, not to make the mistake of taking your athletes' positive behaviors for granted, forgetting to reinforce them for their accomplishments. Athletes have been known to intentionally perform poorly in order to obtain recognition from the coach.

When Should You Reward?

When youngsters are first learning, reward as soon as possible after the correct behavior or its approximation occurs. Once a skill has been learned and as youngsters mature, it is less important to give rewards immediately after the appropriate behavior occurs, with one exception. Athletes low in self-confidence always need to be reinforced soon after making the appropriate response.

Giving rewards when athletes have not earned them also is a mistake. When players have made repeated errors, cost the team a victory, and just had an all-around miserable day, to praise them for some insignificant behavior makes them feel misunderstood and slyly manipulated.

What Type of Reward Should I Use?

Use all three types of rewards listed in Table 5.1, being careful not to overwork any one. These are called *extrinsic* rewards because they come from you or someone else.

Another group of rewards are not directly available for you to use, but they have powerful effects on athletes. These rewards are *intrinsic* to playing the sport. They in-

Table 5.1

Types of Extrinsic Rewards

Tangible rewards	People rewards	Activity rewards
Trophies	Praise	Playing a game rather than doing drills
Medals	Smiles	
Ribbons	Expressions of approval	Being able to continue to play
Decals	A pat on the back	Taking a trip to play another team
Money	Publicity	Getting to take a rest
T-shirts	Expressions of interest	Changing positions with other players

clude such things as athletes' feeling successful, a sense of pride in accomplishment, and feeling competent. Although you cannot directly offer these rewards to your athletes, by belittling them and not recognizing their accomplishments, you can deny them the opportunity to experience these rewards.

Successful coaches place greater emphasis on playing for intrinsic rewards than for extrinsic rewards. Intrinsic rewards are self-fueling, that is, self-satisfaction and pride lead to greater desire to succeed without any extrinsic rewards. Coaches who emphasize extrinsic rewards may find that athletes want ever-increasing amounts until the demand exceeds the supply. The trophies can be only so big; the social recognition can be only so much.

Athletes who play only for extrinsic rewards seldom maintain the long-term motivation that is needed to succeed in athletics. Athletes who most enjoy sports and who excel in them for an extended period of time are motivated primarily by intrinsic rewards.

Extrinsic rewards, however, are *not* useless. All athletes want praise and recognition for their accomplishments. Therefore, coaches should use extrinsic rewards as incentives to athletes to experience the intrinsic rewards and should help athletes understand that intrinsic rewards ultimately are of greatest value.

How Can I Give Positive Reinforcement if the Appropriate Behavior Does Not Occur?

Think small initially. Reward the first signs of behavior which approximate what you want. Then reward closer and closer approximations of the desired behavior. In short, use your reward power to shape the behavior desired.

If you were teaching children who fear the water to swim, you wouldn't expect them to jump into the deep end and begin swimming. Instead, you would begin with a series of small steps, introducing them to the water in the shallow end, getting them to put their face in the water, to learn to float, to glide, to kick, and to breathe. Slowly, with patience and practice, youngsters learn to swim. The same procedure works with many other sports and social skills.

Dealing With Misbehavior

Extinction

Young athletes will misbehave at times; it's only natural. You can respond with a positive or negative approach to this undesirable behavior. One technique of the positive approach is to ignore the behavior. That is, do not reward or punish it. This is called extinction, which can be effective under certain circumstances. In some situations, punishing young people's misbehavior only encourages them to further misbehave because of the recognition they receive for misbehaving. Ignoring such behavior teaches youngsters that unacceptable behavior is not worth anything.

Sometimes, though, you cannot wait for a behavior to fizzle out through nonreward. When young people behave in such a way that they become dangerous to themselves or others, or when it disrupts the activities of others, immediate action is necessary. Youngsters need to be told that the behavior must cease, and if not, that punishment will follow. If the athletes do not stop misbehaving after the warning, punish them.

Extinction does not work well when the misbehavior is self-rewarding. For example, if a youngster kicks you in the shin and you are able to keep from grimacing, he or she still knows that it hurt you. Therein lies the reward. In these circumstances, it is necessary to punish the undesirable behavior.

Extinction works best in situations where young people are seeking recognition through mischievous behaviors, clowning, and grandstanding. Usually, with patience, the failure to get recognition will cause the behavior to disappear.

On the other hand, be alert to not extinguish desirable behavior. When youngsters do something well, they will expect to be positively reinforced. To not

reward them will either cause them to discontinue the behavior or to interpret your silence as negative reinforcement.

Punishment

Some educators say we should never punish our children but should only reinforce their positive behaviors. They argue that punishment does not work, that it creates hostility in youngsters and sometimes develops avoidance behaviors which may be more unwholesome than the origi-

nal problem behavior. It is true that punishment does not always work and that it can create problems when used ineffectively, but when used appropriately, punishment is effective in eliminating undesirable behaviors without creating other undesirable consequences.

Coaches must be able to use punishment effectively because it is impossible to guide young athletes through the use of positive reinforcement and extinction alone. Punishment is part of the positive approach when these guidelines are followed:

1. Use punishment in a corrective way, designed to help athletes improve now and in the future. Do not use punishment to retaliate and make you feel better.

2. When violations of team rules or other misbehaviors occur, impose the punishment in an impersonal way. Do not shout at or scold youngsters because this indicates your attitude is one of revenge.

3. Once a good rule has been agreed upon, ensure that youngsters who violate it experience the unpleasant consequences of their misbehavior. Don't wave the punishment threateningly over their heads. Just do it.

4. A youngster should be given one warning before punishment is delivered.

5. Be consistent in the administration of punishment.

6. Don't pick punishments which cause you to feel guilty. If you cannot think of an appropriate consequence right away, tell the youngster you will think about it and talk with him or her later.

7. Once the punishment is completed, don't make athletes feel they are in the "dog house." If you have dealt with them fairly, and you are comfortable with your decision, make them feel a valued member of the team again.

8. Be certain that what you think is a punishment is not perceived as a positive reinforcement.

9. Never punish athletes for making errors when they are playing.

10. Never use physical activity—running laps or doing push-ups—as punishment. To do so only causes youngsters to resent physical activity, something we want them to learn to enjoy throughout their life.

11. Punish sparingly. Constant use of punishment and criticism causes young athletes to turn their interests elsewhere and to resent you as well.

Key Points to Remember

1. Learning to effectively use the *Principles of Reinforcement* is a valuable communication skill.

2. When the consequence of doing something is positive we tend to do it again, and when the consequence is negative we tend not to do it again. This is the first principle of reinforcement.

3. Reward the performance and not the outcome.

4. Reward athletes more for their effort than for their actual success.

5. Reward the little things along the way toward reaching a goal.

6. Reward not only the learning and performance of sports skills, but also the learning and performance of emotional and social skills.

7. Reward frequently when a youngster is first learning a new skill. Reward occasionally once the skill is well-learned.

8. Reward as soon as possible after the correct behavior or its approximation occurs.

9. Give rewards only when athletes have earned them.

10. Use a variety of extrinsic rewards, being careful not to deny athletes the opportunity to experience the intrinsic rewards of playing.

11. Teach athletes that intrinsic rewards are of greater value than extrinsic rewards.

12. By ignoring athletes' misbehavior when they are seeking attention (extinction), it teaches them that unacceptable behavior is worth nothing.

13. You must learn to use punishment effectively because it is impossible to guide young athletes through the use of positive reinforcement and extinction alone.

CHAPTER 6

Understanding Motivation

When speaking with coaches at workshops or on an informal basis, we are often asked two questions about motivation:

- Why are some athletes so motivated and others so unmotivated?

- How do we motivate our athletes to be the best they can be?

We often answer by asking a question of our own:

- How do we motivate you to be the best coach you can be?

We don't ask this question to beg the issue. Instead, we want coaches to examine their own motives in hopes of discovering a basic principle of motivation:

PEOPLE ARE MOTIVATED
TO FULFILL THEIR NEEDS.

If you understand what your athletes' needs are, and you are able to help them fulfill these needs, you possess the key to their motivation.

You should meet with each of your athletes to learn specifically why he or she has decided to play the sport this season. The more you understand why your athletes are playing the sport, the easier it will be to understand their behavior throughout the season—and to deal effectively with any motivational problems.

Sport psychologists have learned that the two most important needs of young athletes are:

1. To have **fun,** which includes the need for stimulation and excitement, and

2. To feel **worthy,** which includes the need to feel competent and successful. In this chapter, we help you understand how you can help your athletes satisfy these two needs.

Need for Fun

Why do people play—not only sports, but play at all types of things? This question has intrigued philosophers and scientists alike for centuries. Only recently have we begun to know why. Each of us is born with the need for a certain amount of stimulation and excitement, what is often called the need for arousal and what we call fun here.

Optimal Arousal

When our arousal level is too low, we become bored and seek stimulation. We call this "playing" when the primary purpose of the stimulation we seek is to have fun. Sometimes, however, we find ourselves in situations which are more arousing than we would like and we become fearful or anxious. Then we try to decrease our arousal in whatever way is best available.

In other words, people have a need for an optimal amount of arousal—not too little and not too much (see Figure 6.1). This optimal level of arousal differs from person to person. We all know individuals who seem to thrive on a great deal of stimulation and others who are quite content with only a little.

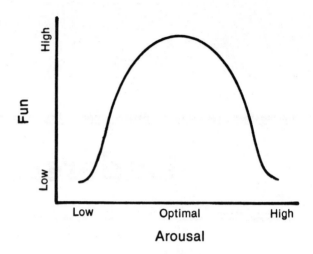

Figure 6.1—Relationship between fun and arousal.

Not only do optimal arousal levels differ from person to person, each of us has periods during the day when we prefer more or less arousal. If you normally have practice in the late afternoon and switch to an early morning practice, you will see what we mean.

The Flow Experience

What makes optimal arousal so desirable? Why do we seek it out? The answer lies in how we feel when experiencing optimal arousal, what one scientist has called the "flow experience." Flow occurs when we are totally immersed in an activity; we lose our sense of time, we feel everything is going just right because we are neither bored nor anxious.

When experiencing "flow" our attention is so intensely centered on the activity that concentration is automatic. When in flow we are not self-critical because our thoughts are totally on the activity. Because we are neither bored nor threatened, we feel in control of ourselves and our environment. One athlete explained it this way: "You are so involved in what you are doing you aren't thinking of yourself as separate from the game."

The flow experience is so pleasing that it

is intrinsically rewarding. We will engage in an activity for no other reason than to experience flow because it is fun. Sports, of course, are popular with young people because they increase arousal to an optimal level, and therefore, are fun. But not always.

For some young people, sports simply aren't fun—they don't increase arousal enough or else they create too much arousal. Coaches are greatly responsible for making sports dull and monotonous or so threatening that athletes feel anxious. Here, then, are some things you can do to help young athletes experience optimal arousal and thus flow.

1. Fit the difficulty of the skills to be learned or performed to the ability of the athletes. The task must be sufficiently dif-

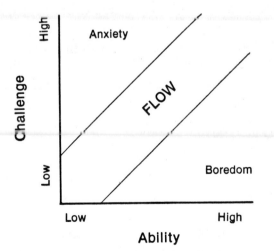

Figure 6.2—Increasing the probability of experiencing flow by matching ability level to the challenge of the task at hand.

ficult to be challenging, but not so difficult that they see no chance of succeeding.

In Figure 6.2 we illustrate this very important point. If athletes' abilities are high but the challenge is low, they will be bored. If athletes' abilities are low and the challenge is high, they will experience anxiety. But if athletes' abilities are reasonably close to the challenge at hand, athletes will experience flow and thus have fun.

2. Keep practices stimulating by using a wide variety of drills and activities for working on skills. Moreover, let the youngsters share in designing some of the activities which will help them learn new skills.

3. Keep everyone active rather than standing around for long periods of time waiting their turn. By following the suggestions presented later in this chapter and in Part 3, you can make practices nearly as much fun as the games. **Note:** Having everyone involved also means involved in the games, not just practice!

4. Avoid constantly instructing during practices and games. Permit your athletes to have some time when they don't have to pay attention to you but can get absorbed in the activity. Constantly yelling instructions from the sidelines during contests does not permit youngsters to experience flow.

5. Do not constantly evaluate your athletes (which we discussed in chapter 4). The flow experience cannot occur when young athletes are continually being

evaluated or made to evaluate themselves—whether the evaluation is positive or negative. There is a time for evaluation, but it is not when the contest is in progress.

In summary, help athletes meet their need for *fun* by making the sport experience challenging and exciting without becoming threatening.

Need to Feel Worthy

We each have a basic need to feel we are competent, to experience some success, to feel we are worthy persons. In our society we quickly learn that our worth depends largely on our ability to achieve. Children as young as 5 years old understand this, and with respect to sports, translate it to mean:

WINNING = SUCCESS

LOSING = FAILURE

Consequently, participation in sports is potentially threatening to young athletes, because they equate their achievement with their self-worth. To win is to be successful, to be competent, to be a worthy person; to lose is to be a failure, to be incompetent, to be unworthy.

When athletes experience a reasonable amount of success it reinforces their sense of competency which, in turn, reinforces their further pursuit of excellence. But if they fail to experience success, athletes may blame themselves for failure and attribute it to a lack of ability. With repeated failure, athletes may decide that if they cannot be certain of success, then at least they will protect their dignity by avoiding failure. Emerging then from early success and failure experiences are two very different types of athletes: one who is motivated to achieve success and another who is motivated to avoid failure.

How Winners Think

Success-oriented athletes engage in drastically different reasoning than failure-oriented athletes about winning and losing. Wendy Winner, a model success-oriented athlete, sees winning as a consequence of her ability, which inspires confidence in her ability to succeed again. When she encounters an occasional failure, Wendy is likely to blame it on insufficient effort; this robs failure of its threat to her self-worth because it doesn't reflect on her ability. To succeed, Wendy believes she simply needs to try harder. Thus, failure increases her motivation rather than reduces it.

For Wendy, an occasional failure is an inevitable part of playing sports and not a fault within herself. Thus she is willing to take reasonable risks of failure—risks that are necessary to achieve success. Wendy and athletes like her direct their energies to the challenges of the sport rather than on worry and self-doubt. They take credit for their success and accept responsibility for their failure. This is a healthy attitude, one you want to foster in your athletes.

How Losers Think

In contrast, meet Larry Loser, a failure-oriented athlete who is filled with self-doubts and anxiety. Larry tends to attribute his failures to a lack of ability and his infrequent success to luck or to his opponents, whom he sees as weak or incompetent. Such thinking produces disaster; Larry blames himself for failure, yet takes little or no credit for his successes.

Athletes like Larry Loser come to believe they are powerless to do anything about their plight because their early experiences in sport have convinced them that no matter how hard they try, the outcome is always the same: failure. They conclude: "Well, trying didn't help, so my problem must be low ability . . . . so why try?"

Because sports so clearly identify winners and losers, failure-oriented athletes like Larry Loser have little choice but to not participate or to maneuver to avoid failure in order to protect their self-worth. Although many such young people choose not to play sports, in Larry's case, parental, coach, and peer pressure keep him playing. Thus, Larry has learned to protect his threatened self-worth by playing the "token effort" game.

Rather than putting forth maximum effort, Larry almost unknowingly gives only token effort so that if he fails he can say he just didn't try hard enough. Why does he do this? Because if he gave maximum effort and failed, others would know he didn't have ability. Not to put forth maximum effort is less threatening, in Larry's thinking, than to have others discover that he lacks ability, which he equates with being unworthy. The tragedy of choosing not to put forth full effort, however, is that it increases his likelihood of failure in his desperate attempt to avoid failure.

But the tragedy becomes even greater. Coaches usually reward effort because it

seems fair—not everyone is skilled, but everyone can try. Yet for Larry Loser, and failure-oriented athletes like him, putting forth full effort risks discovery that he lacks ability, so he doesn't. Failing to do so after encouragement from the coach, leaves the coach puzzled or angered. The coach attributes it to a lack of motivation, but in reality Larry is far from being unmotivated. Instead, he is highly motivated to avoid the threat to his self-worth. It becomes a vicious circle.

Another common ploy of Larry Loser is to keep himself well-armed with excuses. "I was robbed by the ump." "My leg is hurt." "I didn't have the right shoes." "Something got in my eye." "I don't feel good." And on and on.

Coaches who have Larry Losers on the team often will try to solve the problem by arranging some successful experiences for them. But once athletes begin thinking like Larry, they tend to reject success, which mystifies and frustrates coaches even more. Although failure-oriented athletes want to accept success to enhance their self-worth, they reject it because they fear they will be expected to succeed again. They may so fear impending success that they may purposely perform to avoid winning. Not until failure-oriented athletes can learn to accept their own successes is there hope of enhancing confidence in their ability and thus self-worth.

You will find both Wendy Winners and Larry Losers on your team as well as offspring of these types: youngsters who possess varying degrees of both athletes' characteristics. It's especially important that you recognize Larry Loser and those young athletes who tend to be like him, so that you do not misdiagnose their motivational problems. Although the problems of Larry Loser may seem unsolvable, they are not. We will describe a solution shortly.

Self-fulfilling Prophecy

Just as athletes assign reasons to their successes and failures, coaches also assign reasons to their athletes' successes and failures. These reasons—attributions—in turn lead coaches to have certain expectancies of their athletes, which if conveyed, may affect their motivation to perform. Doug's case illustrates how this can occur.

Doug had played basketball satisfactorily last season under Coach Hanson, who frequently encouraged him in practices. This season, playing for a new coach, Mr. Johnson, Doug just couldn't get "untracked." Never being too confident, Doug began attributing his poor playing more and more to a lack of ability. He sensed that Coach Johnson didn't think very much of his ability because he spent little time helping him and encouraged him far less than Coach Hanson had. As his self-doubts increased, he played even worse, and slowly began giving up. After a while, even an occasional good performance and encouragement from Coach Johnson were shrugged off as flukes.

WITH THIS KIND OF MENTAL ATTITUDE FREEMUS... YOU'LL PROBABLY PIN YOURSELF IN TOMORROW'S MATCH!

When Doug failed to respond to his encouragement, Coach Johnson became discouraged with Doug's lack of effort, attributing it to laziness. Finally, in hopes of instilling the missing enthusiasm, Coach Johnson took Doug off the first team and sent him to the second team. Now convinced more than ever that he was worthless, Doug quit the team.

In Doug's case, Coach Johnson clearly told him he had lowered his expectations by sending him to the second team. But coaches often communicate expectancies in more indirect ways. For example, they more often reward those players for whom they have higher expectancies and spend less time with those for whom they hold low expectancies ("Why waste my time with this kid?"). Coaches may have closer relationships with their better players, permitting them to have more input about what the team is doing. Although these messages may be less direct, youngsters easily pick them up.

When these expectancies are conveyed to athletes, they may become self-fulfilling prophecies; that is, athletes may act in ways to fulfill what coaches have prophesied for them. These expectancies-turned-prophecies may, of course, be either positive or negative.

As we would expect, failure-oriented athletes are most vulnerable to negative expectancies. When such athletes, already full of self-doubt, perceive that the coach has low expectations of them, it only affirms what they suspected: "Coach thinks I'm no good so why should I try." When positive expectancies are communicated to failure-oriented athletes they reject them for the same reasons they reject occasional success.

On the other hand, success-oriented athletes—whose self-confidence is strong—most often will reject negative expectancies conveyed by coaches or others. Instead of fulfilling what has been prophesied for them, they will work even harder to show others they are wrong. Positive expectancies, of course, strengthen success-oriented athletes' belief in their own ability.

By now you may be apprehensive as to whether you can do anything positive to influence the motivation of your athletes. The success-oriented athlete seemingly doesn't need to be motivated by you and it seems you can do little to help the failure-oriented youngster. Don't despair, read on!

How Athletes Learn to Fear Failure

Organized sports are very different from the backyard sports most children first learn to play. They have, of course, uniforms and regulation-playing surfaces, rules and of-

ficials to enforce them, spectators and scorekeepers, and you: their coach. But coaches should be aware of some other less obvious differences. These differences are root causes for youngsters learning to fear failure, and understanding these causes will help you appreciate why we prescribe what we do to overcome motivation problems.

Emphasis on Performance, Not Learning

When children are left to themselves to learn sports skills—without coaches, peer pressure, or spectators—they have an ingenious way of avoiding failure. Each time they do not obtain their goal, they simply lower it slightly, learn from their mistake and try again. A few practices and adjustments like these and success is virtually guaranteed.

But they'll never achieve any difficult goals that way, you say? Wrong! When

children do succeed, they naturally tend to raise their goals a little in order to keep the activity challenging. So without adult intervention, children tend to adjust their goals to compromise two opposing forces: the need to set goals low enough to avoid repeated failures and yet high enough to be challenging. The result is that youngsters tend to keep their goals near the upper limits of their current ability. Through this "self-regulated" learning, mistakes are seen as a natural part of the learning process, not as failures.

But when young people begin playing organized sports, the personal evaluation becomes public and official. The emphasis shifts from learning to performing. The mistakes and errors which are a natural part of the learning process may now be misinterpreted as failure to perform.

Unrealistic Goals

Something else happens when youngsters begin playing organized sports. They quickly observe that coaches prefer superior performance and tend to give greater recognition to those athletes who excel. Envious of their superior skills and desirous of similar recognition, the less skilled players attempt to be like the more skilled players. In doing so, these young athletes may set their goals too high for their present level of skill.

And if athletes don't set unrealistically high goals for themselves, sometimes coaches or parents do. Coaches, for example, may set the same performance goal for the entire team, but set it so that it is only within the grasp of the few better athletes. Those parents who vicariously aspire to be stars through their children may also make the mistake of convincing their children to pursue goals which are beyond their reach.

Regardless of whether the coach, parent, or athlete is at fault, the result is the same—unrealistically high goals almost

So what if this guy's the toughest in the state? And he's never been beaten—so what! Your parents and I are counting on you to pin him!

guarantee failure. They cause youngsters to play in order to attain the goals set for them by others, not to meet their own. Tragically, young athletes do not realize such goals are unrealistic; they believe their performance is out of kilter and mistakenly accuse themselves of not having ability and thus being unworthy.

Extrinsic Rewards and Intrinsic Motivation

Third, when young people begin playing organized sports, the sports skills which they have been trying to master for the sheer satisfaction of doing so (intrinsic reward) become subject to an elaborate system of extrinsic rewards. Trophies, medallions, ribbons, plaques, all-star team recognition, and so on may cause a change in why young people play sports—a change that is not desirable. Rather than playing sports primarily for self-satisfaction, youngsters may begin to play primarily to earn these extrinsic rewards. The extrinsic rewards are given not for personal goals, but for attain-

" IS THAT ALL? JUST ANOTHER
MEDAL FOR WINNING THE
STATE CHAMPIONSHIP?! "

ing goals set by others. Once again, the result can be that athletes are influenced to pursue unrealistic goals and doom themselves to failure.

Overemphasis on extrinsic rewards has another negative consequence—it may result in addiction to medals. "Hooked" on the glitter and shine of trophies and medals, such addicted athletes continually want more and bigger rewards to feed their growing habit. When the gold is no longer offered or not within their capability to achieve, they see no value in continuing to participate.

How many athletic "junkies" are there? How often do trophies and medals (extrinsic rewards) undermine athletes' intrinsic motivation to play sports? We don't really know, but it need never happen if we help young athletes understand the meaning of these rewards.

Because extrinsic rewards may undermine intrinsic motivation does not mean that extrinsic rewards should never be given. Extrinsic rewards, properly used, are excellent incentives for motivating youngsters who are struggling to learn sports skills. And, of course, we all like to be recognized for our achievements and to have momentos of past accomplishments.

Our concern is not with the extrinsic rewards as such, but the meaning athletes attach to the rewards. Coaches should constantly let athletes know by word and deed that extrinsic rewards are only tokens of recognition for achieving the larger goal of acquiring and performing sports skills. These tokens do not make one person better than another, they do not guarantee future success, and they are not the primary reason for playing sports. Instead, coaches should help athletes remember that the most important reason for participating in sports is the participation itself. When young athletes understand this message, extrinsic rewards are unlikely to undermine their intrinsic motivation to play the game.

In summary, we have just identified three potential reasons why participation in organized sports may cause young athletes to fear failure.

1. The mistakes and errors that are a natural part of the learning process are misinterpreted as failures.

2. Due to competitive pressures, youngsters set unrealistically high goals which, when not attained, lead the youngsters to conclude that they are failures.

3. Athletes begin to play for extrinsic rewards rather than to attain personal goals.

Enhancing Athletes' Motivation

Most everything we have suggested in previous and forthcoming chapters will directly or indirectly be helpful in enhancing the motivation of your athletes. Your decision to put the well-being of the athlete first and winning second, along with adopting a cooperative rather than a command style, are essential prerequisites. The communication skills we discussed in chapters 3 through 5 also are an integral part of successfully motivating athletes. And we have specified some ways that you can help athletes fulfill their need to have fun. What remains to be done is to find a way to help each young athlete feel worthy. Our goal is a difficult one; we must find a way whereby every athlete can experience success in an environment where actual winners are few and losers are many.

The simple solution is to eliminate losing; in that way, the vicious cycle that produces failure-oriented athletes would never begin. Of course, this is not realistic; besides, learning to lose has positive aspects. The solution lies in changing the way young athletes (and coaches) learn to interpret their losing experiences.

Success is Not Winning

The basic problem is that young athletes learn from parents, coaches, teammates, and the media to gauge their self-worth largely by whether they win or lose. The devastating result of this belief is that athletes can maintain their sense of self-worth only by making others feel unworthy. The most important thing you can do as a coach to enhance the motivation of your athletes is to change this yardstick of success.

Success must be seen in terms of athletes exceeding their own goals rather than surpassing the performance of others. Winning is important, but it becomes secondary to athletes striving to achieve their personal goals.

These personal goals are specific performance or behavioral objectives rather than goals concerning the outcome of winning or losing. The following are examples of personal goals which focus on performance and other behavioral objectives:

• My goal is to jump 6 inches further than last week.

• I want to improve my backhand so that I can control it into either half of the court.

• I want to learn to relax more and enjoy playing.

Setting Realistic Personal Goals

By placing greater emphasis on achieving personal goals, athletes can gain control over an important part of their sport participation—their own success. The important thing here is to set realistic goals, for by doing so athletes ensure themselves a reasonable degree of success. With all the competitive pressures and parental and teammate influence, it is the coach who must help each athlete keep a realistic perspective in setting goals suitable for him or her alone.

MAYBE WE SHOULD START WITH A MORE REALISTIC HEIGHT.

The setting of team goals should not be confused with these personal goals. In fact, team goals are hardly needed if one of the personal goals of each team member is to make the best contribution possible, given his or her current skill level. Setting team goals which state that we want to win "X" number of games or win this or that championship are not useful, and actually undermine the type of personal goals we have just described. Team goals more appropriately deal with learning to play together as a unit, respecting each other, having fun, and playing with good sportsmanship. Accomplishing these team goals and each individual's personal goals is more important than winning. Besides, if athletes achieve these team and individual goals, winning usually takes care of itself.

Consequence of Setting Personal Goals

When winning the game becomes secondary to achieving their own personal goals, athletes are much more motivated to practice. Practices provide athletes with the opportunity to work toward their personal goals with assistance from the coach. Contests are not viewed as the end-all, but as periodic evaluations along the way toward achieving the personal goal. Athletes do not judge themselves as having succeeded or failed on the basis of whether they have won or lost, but in terms of their achievement of the specific performance and behavioral goals they have set.

Evidence from many sources indicates that not only outstanding athletes but those less successful who have most enjoyed and benefited from sport hold this viewpoint. They focus on personal goals, not the defeat of others. The consequence of this viewpoint is incredibly positive.

When athletes are allowed to set their own goals, guided by the coach when necessary to make sure they are realistic, they become responsible for their own progress. They feel in control and take credit for

their successes and responsibility for their failures. As we stated earlier, this is the first step toward helping motivate athletes.

Coaches must possess a great deal of good judgment to help athletes set realistic goals, for they must be able to judge each athlete's present skill level. And this brings up another crucial point, one perhaps you thought about as you read this chapter.

Recognizing An Athlete's Limitations

Athletes do not always perform poorly because they lack motivation. Sometimes it indicates that their personal limits have been reached, that they are performing up to their ability. Neither increased effort nor all the confidence in the world will improve their ability to perform.

Coaches must possess good judgment to help athletes set realistic goals.

Athletes must learn to gracefully accept their limitations, without it destroying their motivation to participate. No one is perfect, yet many athletes are threatened by less than perfect performance, especially when coaches, parents, and teammates make them feel perfection is necessary to feel worthy.

Many athletes need help in learning their limitations without devaluing themselves. Coaches, rather than conveying such nonsense that every athlete is capable of becoming a superstar or professional, will help athletes mature more if they encourage youngsters to seek out and discover for themselves their own limits. Only in this way can athletes learn to maintain realistic goals.

If coaches, however, make athletes believe that they have no limits, that to accept their limits is loathesome, then athletes will be pushed to set unrealistic goals and to eventual failure, or even perhaps personal injury.

Experiencing Success

When coaches help athletes set realistic goals, athletes inevitably experience more success and feel more competent. By becoming more competent, they gain in confidence and can tackle skills of moderate difficulty without fearing failure. They discover that their effort does result in a more favorable outcome and that falling short is most likely caused by insufficient effort. Having realistic goals robs failure of its threat. Rather than indicating that athletes are not worthy, failure indicates they should try harder.

De-emphasize winning and re-emphasize attainment of personal goals. These are the vital steps to enhancing the motivation of all young athletes.

From Motivation to Anxiety

Our concern to this point has been exclusively with maintaining and increasing motivation, because we know being motivated is essential to performing well and enjoying participation. Some coaches wrongly believe the more they can motivate their athletes the better; athletes can be too motivated or too aroused.

Arousal-Performance Relationship

Just as there is an optimal level of arousal for having fun, there is an optimal level of arousal for performing well (see Figure 6.3). When athletes are not sufficiently aroused or when they are too aroused, they will not perform as well as they might; but if they are aroused just the right amount, their performance will be best.

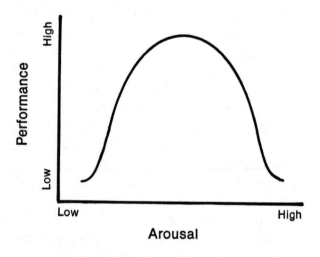

Figure 6.3—Inverted U relationship between arousal and performance.

This optimal arousal level varies, though, for different sports skills. As shown in Figure 6.4, high precision sports skills requiring fine motor control, such as putting in golf, or bowling, are best performed with lower levels of arousal; sports such as basketball and baseball are played better at slightly higher levels of arousal; and skills requiring

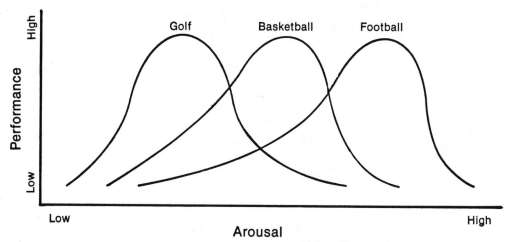

Figure 6.4—Optimal arousal levels for peak performance for different sports.

large muscle movements such as in weight lifting or tackling and blocking in football are better done with even higher levels of arousal. Optimal arousal levels also differ from athlete to athlete. Some athletes better perform a sport skill with considerably less arousal than other athletes.

If some motivation is good, then why isn't more better? When athletes are too motivated or aroused, they become anxious and worried about whether they will be able to succeed—especially failure-oriented athletes. Anxiety causes muscles to become tense, so athletes' movements are not as smooth and easy as when the muscles are most relaxed. Their thoughts shift more to how they are doing rather than concentrating on just doing. Consequently, their attention is not well-centered on the game and they feel out of control.

As you probably recall, these are precisely the opposite conditions necessary for experiencing flow. Athletes perform their best—have their peak performances—when they are in the flow state, which by definition means they are optimally aroused.

Therefore, just as you must help your athletes increase their motivation to an optimal level, you must also help them decrease it when they are too motivated, or anxious. To do so, you need to understand why they become anxious.

Causes of Anxiety

The fundamental cause of anxiety in sports is that athletes become uncertain about whether they can meet the demands which you, their parents, or they place on themselves, when meeting these demands is important to them. The greater the uncertainty athletes have and the more important the outcome is to them, the greater the anxiety.

Some coaches fail to understand this, and instead of helping athletes to feel less uncertain, they make them feel more uncertain. Coaches, for example, will keep athletes uncertain about whether they will make the team or the starting lineup, or get to play at all. Some coaches constantly remind their players about the uncertainty of winning and especially make them feel uncertain about their own individual capabilities. The coach, along with parents and teammates, may also make young athletes feel quite uncertain about their social status or importance on the team. Coaches often create these feelings of uncertainty, not with the intent of making athletes feel anxious, but with the intent of motivating them. Unfortunately, these coaches do not understand the motivation process discussed in this chapter.

Many factors make sports important to

children. As we have already seen, winning itself has a great deal of importance because youngsters link winning with their self-worth. In addition, giving the outcome of the game publicity, adding pagentry to the game, and of course, offering all types of extrinsic rewards increase the game's importance.

Some coaches seem particularly insensitive to the emotional states of athletes, and thus, do not recognize the need to help some youngsters decrease the uncertainty and importance of the game in order to reduce their anxiety. Instead, coaches often feel compelled to give the traditional pregame pep talk. This pep talk typically reminds athletes of the importance of the game and the uncertainties associated with competition. For insufficiently motivated athletes, this pep talk may increase their arousal toward the optimal level. For athletes who are already optimally aroused, this additional "hype" may push them beyond their optimal arousal level, creating anxiety. And for already anxious athletes, it petrifies them!

More than likely, coaches give pep talks out of tradition and to help them alleviate their own anxiety. Unfortunately, in doing so they often do more harm than good. The pep talk fails because it does not address itself to the individual needs of the athletes. Although one athlete may need a coach's oratorical inspiration, another may need reassurance.

You can help overly anxious athletes alleviate their anxiety by finding ways to reduce both the uncertainty about how their performance will be evaluated and the importance they attach to the game. We already have discovered one powerful way to do this. Helping athletes shift their emphasis from winning to achieving their realistic personal goals will go a long way toward removing the threat which causes anxiety. With an emphasis on personal goals, athletes are not attempting to defeat an opponent of uncertain ability, but only to achieve their own performance goals. When youngsters do not link their self-worth to winning and losing, sports are defused of their threat and athletes do not fear failure.

Key Points to Remember

1. Athletes are motivated to play sports to fulfill their need for *fun* and to feel *worthy*.

2. People have a need for an optimal amount of arousal

3. When optimally aroused, the "flow experience" is more likely to occur.

4. You can help athletes experience optimal arousal and thus flow by fitting the difficulty of the skill to the ability of the athlete, keeping practices varied and all players active, and avoiding continually instructing and evaluating your athletes.

5. Sports are potentially threatening to young athletes because they equate their achievement with their self-worth.

6. Success-oriented athletes see winning as a consequence of their ability, blaming failure on insufficient effort.

7. Failure-oriented athletes attribute losing to a lack of ability and infrequent wins to luck, thus blaming themselves for losing and yet not taking credit for winning.

8. Failure-oriented athletes attempt to protect their self-worth by putting forth only token effort so others will not discover their feared lack of ability. Coaches often mistake this lack of effort as a lack of motivation, but in actuality, failure-oriented athletes are highly motivated to avoid the threat to their self-worth.

9. Coaches develop expectancies of athletes which, when conveyed, may become self-fulfilling prophesies.

10. Failure-oriented athletes are most vulnerable to coaches' negative expectancies.

11. Athletes learn to fear failure because:
    a. the mistakes and errors that are a natural part of the learning process are misinterpreted as failures;
    b. competitive pressures result in youngsters setting unrealistically high goals which assure failure; and
    c. athletes begin playing for extrinsic rewards rather than to attain personal goals.

12. The most important thing you can do to enhance your athletes' motivation is to teach them that success means achieving their personal performance goals rather than the performance goals of others.

13. You can play a vital role in helping athletes to set realistic goals. Realistic goals are those that motivate athletes to achieve their finest but to recognize their limitations as well.

14. Athletes perform best when they are optimally aroused or motivated. Too little or too much arousal impairs performance.

15. Optimal arousal differs from skill to skill and from athlete to athlete.

16. Athletes become anxious when they are uncertain about whether they can meet the demands placed on them when meeting these demands is important to them. The greater the uncertainty and the more important the outcome, the greater the anxiety.

17. You can help alleviate athletes' anxiety by decreasing uncertainty and helping to reduce the importance of the outcome.

PART 3

Sport Pedagogy

Pedagogy means teaching, and sport pedagogy refers to the science and art of teaching sports skills—not specific skills such as dribbling, throwing, or tumbling, but the process which coaches use to teach all types of skills. Sport pedagogy is the study of how coaches organize for the season, select and sequence the specific skills they teach, provide verbal instructions, demonstrate skills, and give feedback.

In Part 3, you will learn what we have learned from experienced and skillful coaches and sport scientists about how best to organize and teach sports skills. In chapter 7, we will discuss the preseason planning necessary for a successful season. In chapter 8, we will show you how to decide which sport skills to teach and the sequence in which you should teach them. In chapter 9, we will give you some guidelines for planning and conducting effective practice sessions. Finally, in chapter 10, you will learn how master coaches teach specific sports skills.

CHAPTER 7

Preseason Planning

Meet Coach Befuddled, who earned his name by never planning for an upcoming season. When the first day of practice arrived, confusion—or more accurately chaos—was the order of the day. Let's join Coach Befuddled at his first practice session this year:

"Hey coach, where's the equipment?" asks one youngster.

"I don't know. Didn't Coach Bungle bring it? Where is Coach Bungle?"

Coach Befuddled just assumed his assistant coach, Mr. Bungle, would bring the equipment. He had it at the end of last season, didn't he? He did, but Coach Befuddled forgot to call Mr. Bungle to tell him today is the first practice.

"What do you want us to practice on today?" asks another player.

"Well, uh . . . uh, why don't you kids run a few laps to warm up," replies Coach Befuddled as he gropes to get things going.

"What's the practice and game schedule for the season?" asks one parent.

"Who pays the medical expenses if my child is injured?" another demands.

"What time do I come back to pick up Billy?" asks a third.

Coach Befuddled doesn't have answers to any of these questions because he hasn't planned for the season, let alone the practice. To avoid the organizational problems of Coach Befuddled, read this chapter and use the checklist at the end to organize your preseason planning.

Start A Program

If your community does not have a program for your sport, you may want to start one. Begin by seeking advice from already established groups or from national and state youth organizations which sponsor that sport (see the list of national youth sports agencies in Appendix C). You may also get some help from your city recreation department or local high school coaches and physical education teachers. Once you have their advice, find others who also would be interested in starting a program and call a meeting to get organized. Publicize this meeting through local radio stations and newspapers, and contact the recreation department, schools, YMCA, YWCA, and religious groups in your community.

At your first meeting, you should seek answers to the following questions:

1. Is there sufficient interest in organizing this sport program?

2. How do we best organize ourselves?

3. What will be the goals of the program?

4. How will the program be financed?

5. How will coaches be selected?

6. Where will the team practice?

7. What equipment and supplies will be needed and how will they be obtained?

8. How will the team travel to and from contests?

9. How will medical examinations be arranged for the athletes?

10. How will liability and medical insurance be arranged for the athletes?

Remember—most youth sports programs start through the initiative of one person. If you see the need for a sports program in your community, why not take that initiative so the young members of your community can experience the joys of this sport.

Most youth sports programs start through the initiative of one person.

Preseason Responsibilities

If your community already has an organized program for the sport you want to coach, you first need to let the organization's director know of your interest and qualifications. Once you are selected as a coach, you have a number of responsibilities to fulfill, even before the season begins.

Know Your Organization

Your initial responsibility is to become familiar with the structure and operation of the organization as well as with how it's governed. You should especially become familiar with the organization's goals and its philosophy about youth sports. Speak to program administrators and veteran coaches to find out how things are done. Many organizations hold preseason organizational meetings for their coaches to provide this type of information. And more and more programs are asking coaches to participate in coaching training programs.

Establish Your Philosophy and Style of Coaching

We hope from reading Part 1 that you have already established your coaching philosophy and style. One thing you must consider is whether the organization's goals and philosophy are compatible with yours. If your organization's philosophy is inconsistent with **Athletes First, Winning Second,** then maybe you should introduce the program administrators to *Coaching Young Athletes.*

Prepare the Season's Instructional Outline and Schedule

Preparing a seasonal instructional plan is explained in chapter 8. This plan includes such elements as your goals, the skills and knowledge you plan to teach, and when you plan to teach them.

Prepare a Player Information Form

The sample player information form shown below is an important part of your preseason planning. The information on this form serves not only as a preliminary introduction to your young athletes, but will also be helpful when, for example, you must call your athletes about last-minute scheduling changes or contact their parents in an emergency.

We recommend that the form be reproduced on 5 × 7 cards because they are durable and easy to file. Have each athlete or parent complete the form at your first team meeting.

Plan Registration

Your organization may conduct the registration of athletes for all the teams under its

---

Player Information Form

Name_____ Date of Birth_____

Home Address_____

_____

Home Phone No._____ Height_____ Weight_____

Name of parent or guardian_____

Name and phone number of someone to call if parents are not home_____

_____

School_____ Grade_____

(Other information you think you'll need)_____

_____

_____

'I DON'T UNDERSTAND THIS PART OF YOUR APPLICATION DAVIDSON... BIRTHDAY... STAR DATE - 4.362 ?...

supervision. If, however, you must conduct your own registration, consider the following in your planning.

Publicize registration long before it is to take place through your local newspaper, radio station, and any other popular sources. Select a date and time of day when most individuals will be able to attend, but also provide an opportunity for later registration. Anticipate how many youngsters will show up and recruit a sufficient number of volunteers to assist you. Prepare sufficient copies of forms and handouts for distribution and be sure you have enough pencils on hand.

Registration is a good time to provide athletes and their parents with:

- The goals of your program;

- The schedule and location of games and practices;

- Information about medical expense coverage for injuries;

- Information about equipment your athletes will need to purchase and other costs to parents;

- The date, time, and place of the Parent Orientation Program (to be explained later);

- A request for parent volunteers to help with the program; and

- Your address and telephone number.

Arrange Transportation

First, determine if you'll need to transport your players to practices and games, both in and out of town. If transportation is needed, you should first check with your organization's director to find out if they have transportation procedures and arrangements. If you must arrange or provide transportation yourself, read carefully the discussion about your legal responsibilities presented in chapter 17.

Select a Team Captain

You will also want to decide whether or not to have a team captain. Generally, with athletes under 12, a captain is not needed. With older athletes, however, having one or more captains is often desirable. How many to have depends upon the sport and your situation. Other questions you will want to think about are: (a) how a captain will be selected, (b) what the captain's role will be, and (c) the duration of the captain's tenure. Your philosophy and coaching style will help you answer these questions.

Establish Team Rules

We highly recommend that you establish team rules and penalties for violating them. These will make life easier along the way, both for you and the athletes. Team rules usually are concerned with such things as dress for practice and games, promptness, proper conduct and language, attendance at practice, and the use of alcohol, drugs, and tobacco.

The following are some guidelines for developing team rules:

1. Involve the team in making the rules and penalties, and in understanding the need for them. When the athletes have a part in making the rules, they find it easier to support them and to accept the penalties when they violate them.

2. The rules should be understandable, reasonable, and enforceable.

3. The rules should be short, to the point, and few in number.

4. Try to phrase the rules in a positive way.

5. Remind your athletes of the rules at other times than when they have been violated.

Athletes' parents are instrumental to the success of a youth sports program.

Plan Your Parent Orientation Program

The success of many sports programs is determined in part by the cooperation of the athletes' parents. When problems arise between parents and coaches, it frequently stems from a lack of understanding and inadequate communication. Many of these problems can be avoided if coaches take the time to meet with parents prior to the season

in what we call a Parent Orientation Program. Chapter 18 presents a detailed description of the purposes and procedures for conducting a Parent Orientation Program.

Prepare Instructional Aids and Materials

Instructional aids and materials which can help you teach the skills of your sport are available. Sequence pictures, film loops, and videotapes of how to perform a skill; diagrams of offensive plays or drills; bulletin boards and chalkboards; pull buoys for learning to swim; tumbling belts for learning to perform somersaults; kickboards for soccer; blocking dummies for football; and baseball batting tees are just some examples of these aids. In some cases, you may need to order materials months before the season begins, so plan to obtain them well in advance.

Plan for Practices and Games

Some of the major practice and game details for which you may be responsible are:

1. Scheduling the days and times of practice sessions and games;

2. Scheduling the facilities for the season;

3. Scheduling your officials for the games;

4. Arranging for the preparation of the playing area (e.g., cleaning and taping wrestling mats, lining the baseball field) for practice sessions and games;

5. Establishing procedures for inclement weather practice for outdoor sports; and

6. Arranging for protection of valuables during practice sessions and games.

Select Your Assistant Coaches

If you have a large number of athletes on your team, you probably will need one or more assistant coaches. Select your assistants carefully; they will be a reflection of you and your program. Of course, we recommend that each of your assistants reads *Coaching Young Athletes* and that you discuss with them the contents of this book.

Your assistant coaches should have a philosophy and coaching style consistent with yours. Nothing but turbulent times lie ahead if you are a cooperative style coach and your assistant is a command style coach.

Select your coaches also on the basis of skills which complement but not necessarily duplicate yours. Also of considerable important is selecting assistant coaches with whom you enjoy working. Coaching is suppose to be *fun*.

Plan With Your Assistant Coaches

Before the season, you should meet with your assistant coaches to go over everything presented in this chapter that you think is relevant—from your philosophy and style of coaching to safety precautions that should be taken during practice sessions. As you plan with your assistants, give each of them specific responsibilities at practices and games. Discuss the language, conduct, and appearance that you expect from them in front of the athletes. Encourage them to discuss, question, and give input into your preliminary organizational efforts and throughout the season. You all should leave this meeting having come to an agreement on how the entire program will be conducted.

Plan for a Postseason Evaluation

Plan for an evaluation of your program at the end of the season by your athletes, assistant coaches, and parents. Have parents complete the Parent Evaluation Form on page 185. Meet with your assistant coaches and athletes to evaluate the season and make notes of their observations. If you don't think your athletes feel comfortable about evaluating you honestly, ask them to write their comments (if they are old enough) and give them to you anonymously.

Acquire Liability Insurance

If your organization has no liability coverage, we recommend that you obtain such coverage to protect yourself. You will understand why after you read chapter 17, "You and the Law." Your policy should provide coverage for such things as (a) the occurrence of bodily injury or damages on the premises where you are coaching, (b) personal injury liability, which includes protection against acts of negligence, and (c) nonowned car liability in a situation in which volunteers are using their own cars at your request or one of your athletes is driving his or her car or another car at your request. One inexpensive source of liability insurance is in the form of a "business pursuits" clause added to either a homeowner's or renter's insurance policy.

Preseason Planning Checklist

To help you remember all the things you need to plan for, we have prepared a "Preseason Planning Checklist." We also have included some items in the checklist which were not discussed in this chapter but are discussed in other parts of this book.

_____ Know the structure and operation of your youth sport organization.

_____ Establish your philosophy and style of coaching (see chapters 1 and 2).

_____ Prepare an instructional outline and schedule for the season (see chapter 8).

_____ Prepare a player information form.

_____ Plan registration.

_____ Arrange transportation for the athletes.

_____ Plan for the selection of a team captain.

_____ Establish team rules and penalties with your team.

_____ Plan a parent orientation program.

_____ Prepare and obtain instructional aids and materials.

_____ Schedule days and times of practices and games.

_____ Schedule facilities for practices and games.

_____ Schedule officials for games.

_____ Arrange for the preparation of the playing area for practice sessions and games.

_____ Establish inclement weather practice procedures for outdoor sports.

_____ Arrange for protection of valuables during practice.

_____ Select assistant coaches and plan the season with them.

_____ Plan for a postseason evaluation of your program.

_____ Arrange for your athletes to have medical examinations (see chapter 14).

_____ Plan a conditioning program (see chapter 12).

_____ Know how accident expenses are covered.

_____ Know what to do in case of an accident (see chapter 15).

_____ Plan proper safety procedures.

_____ Obtain personal liability insurance if you are not protected.

CHAPTER 8

Preparing Your Instructional Outline for the Season

An instructional outline is an organized plan of everything that you would like to teach in the upcoming season: for example, sport skills, rules, sportsmanship, and strategies. This outline is as important to a coach as a blueprint is to an architect. In this chapter, we will take you through the following three steps which will help you prepare your instructional outline for the season.

Step 1
Establish Your Instructional Goals

Step 2
Select the Subject Matter to Include in your Outline

Step 3
Organize the Subject Matter for Instruction

Step 1
Establish Your Instructional Goals

Planning a journey is impossible unless you know where you are going. Likewise, preparing your instructional outline is impossible unless you know your instructional goals. These goals should be compatible with you and your organization's philosophy and the objectives you selected in chapter 2.

But what are instructional goals? They are general statements of what you hope your athletes will know or be able to do at the end of the season. These statements

Table 8.1

Examples of Instructional Goals for Two Sports

Novice Wrestling (Ages 10-13)	Advanced Soccer (Ages 13-15)
The wrestlers will be able to demonstrate: 1. Mastery of the fundamental wrestling skills necessary to successfully participate in practices and matches at a novice level. 2. Knowledge of proper nutritional and safe weight control practices and ability to apply it to themselves. 3. Accurate and complete knowledge of basic rules of the sport. 4. Appropriate sportsmanship behaviors in practices and matches. 5. Knowledge and application of the basic strategies needed to effectively participate in matches at the novice level.	The soccer players will be able to demonstrate: 1. Mastery of advanced individual soccer skills necessary to participate in games at this level. 2. Acquisition of the offensive and defensive patterns of team play needed to successfully participate in games at this level. 3. Appropriate sportsmanship behaviors in practices and games. 4. Development of positive personal qualities in practices and games.

should be written so that you will be able to verify that an athlete has achieved them. They should be written to conform to three criteria and to indicate:

Criterion 1: that the performance can be observed and, if necessary, measured;

Criterion 2: the general standard for determining when the goal is achieved; and

Criterion 3: the performance and the conditions under which it is to occur.

An example of an instructional goal and an analysis of it in terms of the above criteria is as follows: The basketball players will be able to demonstrate (Criterion 1) that they have mastered (Criterion 2) the offensive and defensive patterns of play in practice and game situations (Criterion 3).

In Table 8.1, we have listed two sets of instructional goals. The first set is for a novice wrestling team of 10- to 13-year-olds and

the second is for an advanced soccer team of 13- to 15-year-olds. We purposely selected an individual and team sport and novice and advanced groups for your comparison.

You should notice two things about these goals. First, coaches teach much more than

just the technique of the sport. And second, none of the goals pertain to winning.

Now try writing your own instructional goals or adapting those in Table 8.1 to your situation. You should end up with about six goals or less. If you have many more than six, you probably have made them too specific and they will need to be revised. Remember that instructional goals are general statements.

Before you prepare the final version of your instructional goals, meet with as many of your team members and assistant coaches as possible to get their opinion of them. Remember, cooperative style coaches share the decision making. How much you can share with your athletes depends, of course, on their maturity, but you should share what you can.

With the input from your athletes and assistant coaches, prepare a final version of your instructional goals. Use these goals in three ways. First, be sure to review them with your team at the beginning of the season and periodically thereafter. Second, give them to parents, assistant coaches, and others who might be interested so that they too know what you wish to achieve. And third, use them to begin the next step: selecting the subject matter.

Step 2
Select the Subject
Matter for Your Outline

The subject matter you select to teach to your athletes should come from your instructional goals. For each goal, ask yourself: What will the athletes need to learn in order to achieve this instructional goal? This will give you a list of the things you think your athletes need to learn.

Developing these lists is a vital part of your preparation for the season. To help you, we have developed samples of subject matter for the different goals in Table 8.1 and listed them in Tables 8.2 through 8.9. We encourage you to adapt the information in these tables to your own situation.

Once you have selected the subject matter for each goal, you need to determine if each item is appropriate for the athletes on your team. This is a difficult task if you have had little coaching experience, but you can get help in a couple of ways. First, you can seek the advice of more experienced coaches or physical education teachers. Ask them to identify what most athletes in the age level you are coaching have been ready to learn. Second, evaluate the subject matter you have selected with the following checklist.

Evaluating Your
Subject Matter

☐ Is the skill reasonably safe?

☐ Do the athletes have the physical strength to perform the skill?

☐ Do the athletes have sufficient motor coordination to begin learning the skill?

☐ If the skill requires lead-up skill training, have the athletes mastered these skills?

☐ Does the subject matter contribute to the instructional goal more effectively than another possible choice?

☐ Are the athletes interested in learning the subject matter; if not, can enthusiasm for learning it be generated at this age level?

☐ Is the subject matter accurate?

☐ Do the athletes have sufficient emotional and intellectual maturity to begin learning the subject matter?

If the answer to any of these questions is NO, replace or eliminate the item from the list.

Table 8.2

Individual Skills Selected to Achieve Wrestling Goal 1

> **Goal 1**
> The wrestlers will be able to demonstrate they have mastered the fundamental wrestling skills necessary to successfully participate in practices and matches at a novice level.

Individual Skills

Takedowns

1. Do's and Don'ts
2. Tie Ups
3. Double Leg
4. Single Leg
5. Arm Drag
6. Fireman's Carry
7. Duck Under

Counters to Takedowns

1. Defense on your feet
2. Hip Block
3. Whizzer
4. Cross Face
5. ¼ Nelson
6. Pancake

Escapes and Reversals

1. Referee's Starting Position
2. Do's and Don'ts
3. Stand Up
4. Sit Back, Turn In
5. Hip Roll
6. Switch

Counters to Escapes and Reversals

1. Counter to Stand Up
2. Counter to Sit Back, Turn In
3. Counter to Hip Roll
4. Counter to Switch

Breakdowns and Rides

1. Do's and Don'ts
2. Cross Face-Near Leg
3. Far Ankle-Knee Bump
4. Far Ankle-Waist
5. Two on One Ride

Counters to Breakdowns and Rides

1. Counter to Cross Face-Near Leg
2. Counter to Ankle-Knee Bump
3. Counter to Far Ankle-Waist
4. Counter to Two on One Ride

Pinning Combinations

1. Half Nelson
2. Cross Face Cradle
3. Arm Bar-Reverse Half
4. ¾ Nelson

Counters to Pinning Combinations

1. Regaining a Base
2. Counter to Half Nelson
3. Counter to Arm Bar
4. Counter to Cradle
5. Counter to ¾ Nelson

Table 8.3

Nutrition and Weight Control Knowledge Selected to Achieve Wrestling Goal 2

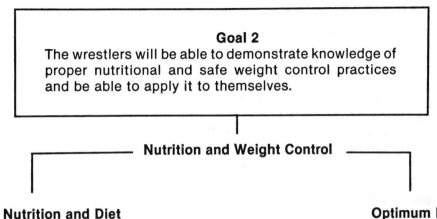

Goal 2
The wrestlers will be able to demonstrate knowledge of proper nutritional and safe weight control practices and be able to apply it to themselves.

Nutrition and Weight Control

Nutrition and Diet

1. Need for proper nutrition

2. Elements of a balanced diet

   a. Milk group
   b. Meat group
   c. Vegetable-fruit group
   d. Bread-cereal group

3. Meal composition and performance

   a. Carbohydrates
   b. Fats
   c. Proteins
   d. Sugars
   e. Vitamins
   f. Minerals

4. Size and timing of meals relative to exercise or competition

   a. Pre- and post-practice
   b. Pre- and post-match
   c. Tournament

5. The need for water

   a. Water as body-building material
   b. Water as a regulator of body process

6. Use of drugs and their effect on health and performance

   a. Coffee
   b. Tea
   c. Alcohol
   d. Smoking
   e. Other drugs

Optimum Body Weight

1. How to estimate it

   a. Age
   b. Body surface area
   c. Growth level
   d. Amount of physical activity

2. How to achieve it and maintain it over a season

   a. Balanced diet
   b. Proper amount of physical activity

3. Discourage the practice of fluid deprivation and dehydration to "make weight"

   a. Rubber suits
   b. Steam rooms
   c. Saunas
   d. Hot boxes
   e. Laxatives
   f. Diuretics

4. Physiological consequences and medical complications resulting from fluid deprivation, dehydration, and food restriction

Table 8.4

Basic Rules Selected to Achieve Wrestling Goal 3

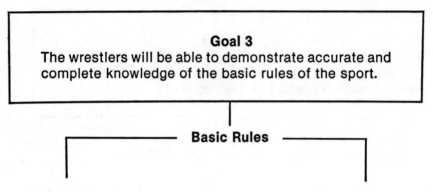

Goal 3
The wrestlers will be able to demonstrate accurate and complete knowledge of the basic rules of the sport.

── **Basic Rules** ──

Illegal Holds

1. Full Nelson
2. ¾ Nelson
3. Figure 4 scissors
4. Back Souplesse
5. Hammerlock
6. Toe and Finger Holds
7. Front Head Lock
8. Body Slam
9. Twisting Knee Lock
10. Strangle Holds

Match Procedures

1. Length of periods
2. Rest periods
3. Start of periods
4. Weight classes
5. Time of fall
6. Injury time out
7. Uniform
8. Headgear
9. Minimum time between bouts
10. Coaching during wrestling
11. Stalling
12. The wrestling area and out-of-bounds

Scoring of Holds

1. Takedown
2. Reversal
3. Escape
4. Near fall
5. Riding time

Team Scoring for Dual Meets

1. Fall
2. Decision
3. Draw

Table 8.5

Sportsmanship Behaviors Selected to Achieve Wrestling Goal 4

> **Goal 4**
> The wrestlers will be able to demonstrate appropriate sportsmanship behaviors in practices and matches.

Sportsmanship Behaviors

1. Demonstrates proper control of emotions.

2. Demonstrates use of appropriate language.

3. Is courteous to opponents, teammates, officials, coaches, and parents.

4. Is humble in winning and gracious in defeat.

5. Respects opponent as a person in winning and losing.

6. Abides by the rules of wrestling and never intentionally uses questionable holds or attempts to punish an opponent.

Table 8.6

Basic Strategies Selected to Achieve Wrestling Goal 5

> **Goal 5**
> The wrestlers will be able to demonstrate knowledge and application of basic strategies needed to effectively participate in matches at the novice level.

Basic Strategies

1. Concentrates attack on opponent's weaknesses and forces opponent to wrestle his way.

2. Wears opponent down with tactics that depend on leverage, weight, and skill rather than brute force.

3. Fakes and sets opponent up before driving hard with the move.

4. When taking an opponent to the mat, the wrestler lands in a good position relative to his opponent with weight on opponent.

5. Looks for opportunities to pin after a takedown or reversal because the opponent is usually caught off balance in these situations.

6. Immediately after a takedown, the wrestler ties opponent up into a ride before starting an offense.

7. Always tries to react more quickly than opponent from referee's position.

8. When opponent is about to get out of a ride, switches immediately to another ride.

9. Always breaks opponent down before attempting a pin hold.

10. Never gets overanxious to pin opponent when he is fresh and strong.

Table 8.7

Advanced Individual Skills Selected to Achieve Soccer Goal 1

> **Goal 1**
> The soccer players will be able to demonstrate they have learned the advanced individual soccer skills necessary to participate effectively in games at this level.

Advanced Individual Skills

Kicks

1. Pivot instep
2. Sole of foot
3. Heel

Heading

1. As a method of passing
2. To score a goal
3. To bring the ball to the ground
4. To clear from own goal area

Dribbling

1. Speed dribbling
2. Changing speed and direction
3. Feinting

Defense

1. Marking an opponent without the ball
2. Marking an opponent with the ball
3. Front block tackle
4. Sliding tackle
5. Shoulder tackle

Receiving

1. Instep
2. Inside of foot
3. Outside of foot
4. Head

Table 8.8

Advanced Patterns of Team Play Selected to Achieve Soccer Goal 2

Goal 2
The soccer players will be able to demonstrate they have acquired the advanced offensive and defensive patterns of team play needed to effectively participate in games at this level.

Advanced Patterns of Team Play

Offensive Attacks

1. Short passing
2. Long passing
3. Use of both short and long passing attacks in a game

Offensive Formations

1. "W"
2. 4-2-4
3. 4-3-3

Offensive Set Plays

1. Kick off
2. Throw-in
3. Corner kick
4. Goal kick
5. Free kick

General Types of Defense

1. Zone
2. Man-for-man
3. Combination of zone and man-for-man

Types of Specific Defense

1. At midfield
2. Around the goal
3. Against the short passing game
4. Against the long passing game
5. Against the "W" formation
6. Against the 4-2-4 formation
7. Against the 4-3-3 formation

Defense Against Set Plays

1. Kick off
2. Throw-in
3. Corner kick
4. Goal kick
5. Free kick

Table 8.9

Positive Personal Qualities Selected to Achieve Soccer Goal 4

> **Goal 4**
> The soccer players will be able to demonstrate they have developed positive personal qualities in practices and games.

Positive Personal Qualities

1. Enthusiasm and a positive attitude toward the game and toward participation.

2. Self-discipline in training and practices.

3. Self-confidence as a result of personal accomplishments.

4. Perseverence in meeting all the challenges of practicing to play the game and actually playing it.

5. Emotional control in "pressure" or "difficult" situations that occur in practices and games.

6. Cooperation in playing together with members of the team.

7. Dedication and loyalty to the team and its goals.

8. Competitive attitude in practices and games.

9. Industriousness and the desire to practice and strive for perfection.

10. Ability to conform to the rules of the team.

Now that you have selected the subject matter for the upcoming season, you need to determine how much your athletes realistically can learn. Although you may want to teach everything on your list, any of the following five factors may prevent you from doing so: (a) total amount of practice time available, (b) ratio of athletes to coaches on the team, (c) readiness levels of your athletes, (d) learning rates of your athletes, or (e) facilities and equipment available. Let's look more closely at how each of these factors may influence what your athletes can learn in a season.

Practice Time

Can your athletes learn all the subject matter you have selected in the amount of time available? No formula will provide you with an exact answer to this question. You will have to use your good judgment. We will give you some help, though, in answer-

"IF WE PRACTICE 4 HOURS A DAY, 6 DAYS A WEEK I THINK WE CAN LEARN ALL THESE SKILLS BY THE YEAR 2000!"

ing this question in Step 3, where we discuss the instructional schedule for the season.

It is probably best to select a little more subject matter than you think your youngsters can learn in a season. Then you will always be prepared with new material when the youngsters are ready to learn more. Keep in mind, however, that just because you have selected a certain amount of material for the season does not mean you must teach all of it. It is far better for your athletes to learn a few things well than to master nothing.

Ratio of Athletes to Coaches

If you have 25, 30, or more athletes on your team and no assistant coaches, you will have great difficulty teaching all the subject matter your athletes could learn. Although an ideal ratio of athletes to coaches depends on the sport, we recommend a ratio of about 10 athletes to 1 coach for most sports. Remember that if you have assistant coaches, more learning will occur only when each of them is an effective teacher and when all of you are well-organized and have carefully planned each practice session.

Readiness Levels

Your athletes' level of development will determine, in part, whether they are ready to learn a particular item. Their level of development depends upon:

1. The traits which they inherit and the rate at which these traits unfold (maturation rate), and

2. Their prior experiences, especially previously learned behavior.

When learning skills, children tend to follow a predictable pattern of development,

YOU MEAN YOU GUYS DON'T UNDER-
STAND A SIMPLE PLAY LIKE THIS?

proceeding from simple to complex skills. The *rate of maturation,* however, differs considerably among children, which is why all youngsters are not ready to learn the same sport skill at the same age. For this reason, it is wise to evaluate the different skill levels of your athletes so that you can select those sport skills for which your athletes will be ready. You should conduct the evaluation at one of the first few practice sessions. Simply ask the athletes to perform the basic skills you think they should have in their repertoire and then observe and record their performance.

Learning Rates

The amount of material that can be learned in a season will vary among children because they learn at different rates. Thus, some children will master a great amount of material and others will master much less. One way to prepare for different learning rates is to plan to teach a little more material than you think your better athletes can learn in a season. Then, individualize your instruction by adjusting the content and approach to the unique characteristics of each athlete. We will show you how to do this in Step 3.

Facilities and Equipment

The facilities and equipment available can also influence the amount of material that your athletes can learn. For example, athletes will obviously develop more shooting skills practicing in a gymnasium with six baskets rather than in a gymnasium with only two. Likewise, having eight basketballs for each practice will encourage greater development than having only one.

Although you can usually do little to improve your facility, at least for the immediate season, you can frequently improve your equipment situation. For example, if you have only a few basketballs or soccer balls, ask those athletes who have their own balls to bring them to practice or ask local businesses to make donations toward the purchase of much needed equipment. In most cases, improving your equipment is a matter of being resourceful.

Step 3
Organize the Subject Matter for Instruction

Once you have selected the subject matter to achieve your instructional goals, you need to organize it into an instructional schedule for the season. A complete instructional schedule includes all of the subject matter you selected in Step 2.

An example of how to organize the skills selected to achieve the first wrestling goal (see Table 8.2) into an instructional schedule for the season based on two practices a week is shown in Table 8.10. The schedule of skills to be taught (T) and practiced (P) at each practice session, in the example, forms a systematic instructional sequence, indicating what to teach and practice as well

Table 8.10

Partial Instructional Schedule for Wrestling Goal 1

Goal 1: The wrestlers will be able to demonstrate they have mastered the fundamental wrestling skills necessary to successfully participate in practices and matches at a novice level.

Skills	Month 1								Month 2				...etc.	Time (in minutes) Spent on Each Skill for the Season
	Week 1 T	Week 1 TH	Week 2 T	Week 2 TH	Week 3 T	Week 3 TH	Week 4 T	Week 4 TH	Week 1 T	Week 1 TH	Week 2 T	Week 2 TH	...etc.	
Takedowns														
1. Do's & Don'ts	T(10)	P(10)	P(5)						P(5)					30
2. Tie Ups	T(15)	P(10)	P(10)							P(10)		P(10)		55
3. Double Leg			T(15)	P(15)	P(10)			P(10)		P(10)		P(10)		70
4. Single Leg						T(15)	P(15)	P(10)		P(10)		P(10)		60
													Total Time	215
Counters to Takedowns														
1. Defense on Feet	T(15)	P(10)	P(5)					P(10)						40
2. Hip Block								T(15)	P(10)	P(10)				35
3. Whizzer									T(10)	P(10)				20
4. Cross Face										T(10)		P(10)		20
													Total Time	115
Escapes & Reversals														
1. Referee's Starting Position		T(10)	P(5)											15
2. Do's & Don'ts		T(10)	P(5)	P(5)					P(5)					25
3. Stand Up		T(10)	P(15)	P(10)	P(10)		P(10)				P(10)			65
4. Switch					T(15)	P(15)	P(10)				P(10)			50
													Total Time	155
. . .													. . .	
etc.													etc.	

Note:
T(10) = Teach skill for the first time in 10 minutes
P(10) = Practice or drill the skill as a team for 10 minutes
  As the season progresses, individual practice time should be built into your instructional schedule so that your athletes can practice what they would like.

as when to do so. This schedule should be repeated for all of your goals.

To develop an instructional schedule, you should begin by ordering the skills within each category; the more basic skills are listed first and the more complex listed last. This will be the order in which you should teach these skills. For example, in Table 8.2, under the category "Escapes and Reversals," Referee's Starting Position and Do's and Don'ts are the basic skills that should be taught before the Stand Up. The instructional schedule should also include the amount of time you plan to spend on each skill (a) at each practice session, (b) for each week, (c) for each month, and (d) for the entire season.

At first glance, your instructional schedule may seem to be a rigid format that is insensitive to the individual learning rates of your athletes or their personal learning goals. This need not be the case if you do the following:

1. Build into your instructional schedule a certain amount of time at each practice session for your athletes to practice the skills of their choice.

2. Change your instructional schedule at any time during the course of the season when it is not meeting the needs of your athletes.

3. Don't expect all your athletes to learn all of the skills you have listed in your schedule. The number of skills an athlete masters will depend upon his or her present skill level and inherited ability to learn new skills.

If you are a veteran coach, you will be able to put together a realistic instructional schedule. If you are a beginning coach, we recommend you seek the advice of more experienced coaches or physical education teachers. This will increase your chance of constructing a realistic schedule right from the outset.

Constructing an instructional schedule is a lot of work, but you only have to do it once prior to the start of the season. After you have tried it and revised it once, you probably will not have to make any major changes in it for future seasons. Thus, in the long run, it will save you preseason planning time.

Key Points for Preparing an Instructional Outline for the Season

STEP 1: Establish Your Instructional Goals

• Write your instructional goals so they are compatible with your organization's philosophy and your objectives and style of coaching.

I THINK WE SHOULD CUT BACK A TAD ON THE 'BALLET COORDINATION' TRAINING...

• Write your instructional goals so you will be able to verify that they have been achieved.

• Share your instructional goals with your assistant coaches, the team, parents, and others who might have an interest in them.

STEP 2: Select the Subject Matter to Include in Your Outline

• The subject matter selected should come from your instructional goals by asking what the athletes need to learn in order to achieve each of these goals.

• Determine if the subject matter you've selected is appropriate for the athletes on your team.

• Estimate how much of the subject matter you will be able to teach in the upcoming season.

STEP 3: Organize the Subject Matter for Instruction

• For each of your goals, develop an instructional schedule which will indicate what to teach and practice as well as when to do so.

CHAPTER 9

Preparing for a Practice

Having a plan for the season won't be much help unless you know what is involved in preparing for a single practice. Your goal is simple—to have practices which are well organized, safe, fun, and enable your athletes to learn and remember all that you teach. In this chapter, we will show you how to attain this goal, or more accurately, how you can work toward attaining it.

Planning for a Typical Practice

Many coaches show up at practice with only a vague idea of what they will practice, or perhaps, with no idea at all. Obviously, a well-planned practice will be more effective. And as you learned in chapter 8, planning each practice without a master plan for the season—an instructional schedule—is not effective planning either. The instructional schedule makes planning easier and provides continuity in planning from one practice to the next.

As you prepare for each practice look at your instructional schedule to see what skills you had planned to teach and how much time you had planned to spend teaching and practicing them. Also, take into account the events of the previous practice(s)—what you observed and what your athletes and assistant coaches told you. Then adjust your practice plan to accommodate all these factors.

You may have to revise your instructional schedule during the season depending upon how your athletes are progressing. After the practice plan is designed, but before the practice begins, meet with your assistant coaches and review it so that everyone knows their responsibilities during the practice.

Now let's focus on the practice plan itself. To give you an idea of how a typical practice is organized, we have outlined a sample plan for a 1½-hour session. This plan is presented only as a guide to help you design your own practice plans.

Sample Plan
For a Practice

Date:

Performance Objectives:

Equipment:

Time Schedule and Parts of Practice:

    4:00 - 4:10   Warm-up

    4:10 - 4:30   Practice previously taught skills

    4:30 - 4:55   Teach and practice new skills

    4:55 - 5:25   Practice under competitive conditions

    5:25 - 5:30   Coach's comments

Evaluation of the Practice:

Let's examine each of the elements of this plan more closely.

Date

Record the date so you know when you taught and practiced certain material. This will help after the season when you are evaluating and revising your instructional schedule.

Performance Objectives

We strongly recommend that you have performance objectives for each of your practices. These objectives are specific statements of what you want the athletes to know or be able to do as a result of this particular practice session.

Do not confuse performance objectives with instructional goals. Instructional goals are general statements of what the athletes should know or be able to do as a result of your coaching over the course of the entire season. A performance objective is more specific than an instructional goal.

Your performance objectives will come from your instructional schedule. Which ob-

"DON'T WORRY COACH, IT'LL ALL COME CLEAR IN TIME."

jectives you select for a particular practice session will depend upon where you are in your instructional schedule and what is scheduled to be taught and practiced at that time. Using Table 8.10, for example, if it is Tuesday of Week 3 of Month 1, your objectives should be written so that they focus on teaching the "switch" for the first time and practicing two previously taught skills, the "stand up" and the "double-leg takedown."

Performance objectives are written like instructional goals, only much more specifically. They should be written:

1. In observable and measurable terms;

2. To indicate the conditions under which the performance is to occur;

3. To include the standard stating when the objective is achieved.

Examples of performance objectives are:

1. The athletes will be able to takedown their opponent, who is offering mild resistance, at least 5 out of 7 times using a single-leg takedown from a wrist tie-up.

2. The athletes will be able to perform a "throw in" three consecutive times according to the rules of soccer during the "throw in" drill in practice.

3. The athletes will be able to make at least 7 lay-ups out of 10 attempts with their nondominant hand during the lay-up drill in basketball practice.

4. The athletes will be able to execute at least 3 sacrifice bunts out of 6 attempts during the bunting drill in baseball practice.

Equipment

List the equipment (e.g., mats, balls, bats) needed to conduct the practice. Prior to the actual practice, check the equipment you plan to use to be certain it is safe, clean, and operational. Also, remember to bring it to practice!

Time Schedule and Parts of Practice

Using a time schedule will help you make efficient use of your time. Without it you will find you have not accomplished much of what you set out to do. You should not, however, be afraid to adjust the schedule as practice proceeds. The athletes may need more practice time to master a difficult skill than what you allocated. Or everybody may seem stale, so you will have to try to inject something new to motivate them.

The time schedule shown in the Sample Plan is quite common, but can be varied depending upon how much time you want to spend on a particular part of the practice. The usual parts of a practice session and the order in which they typically occur are also shown in this plan. Although on occasion you may not use all of these parts or use them in the order shown, most of the time you will want to follow the time schedule and parts shown in the Sample Plan.

Warm-up

The importance of warming-up cannot be overemphasized. We discuss the physiological purpose of the warm-up in chapter

---

Every practice should begin with appropriate warm-up exercises.

---

12 and its function in injury prevention in chapter 14. Every practice should begin with appropriate warm-up exercises.

Practice Previously Taught Skills

Skills that were taught previously, especially those which the team needs to improve on, should be practiced during this time period. This part of practice is usually devoted to practicing skills in the form of drills you have designed. These drills should be (a) fun and safe to perform, (b) designed so that they are consistent with the practice principles discussed later in this chapter, and (c) effective for learning the skill. It is a good idea to occasionally let your team help design some of the drills. Whatever you do, *don't drill so much that it becomes monotonous.*

Prior to having the team practice a skill, review the key points and strategy of performing the skill and give a demonstration if necessary. Once the youngsters have been reminded how to perform the skill and also understand how to proceed with the drill,

arrange them so that they can begin practicing. As they are practicing, move from one youngster to another giving effective feedback according to step 4 in chapter 10.

It is also a good idea to set aside some time in this period for the youngsters to individualize their practice. Simply have them practice those skills on which they need more work. Allow them to practice these skills any way they would like, provided it is safe and effective for learning. Again, provide each young athlete with effective feedback while they are practicing.

Teach and Practice New Skills

The four steps for teaching a new skill will be presented in chapter 10, so we will not repeat them here. The procedures for practice should be designed in accordance with the practice principles presented later in this chapter.

Practice Under Competitive Conditions

This part of the practice session should finish on a "high note" and be devoted to practicing the skills learned in simulated "contest" conditions. This does not mean, however, that your team should be left unsupervised or practicing without a purpose. On the contrary, you should direct and control their play in simulated "contest" conditions toward accomplishing specific performance objectives. Such direction and control, however, should not be overbearing.

Coach's Comments

Use this part of the practice session to comment on how the team practiced. Direct your comments to the whole team rather than to a particular athlete. Tell them what they still need to improve upon. Compliment them for their effort and for what they performed correctly. You may want to ask your young athletes to evaluate the practice session and offer suggestions for improvement. This is also a good time to briefly discuss what you plan to do at the next practice session. You may even ask for suggestions from the team. Finally, inform the team of the time and place of the next practice session as well as anything else that is important for them to know before the next session.

Evaluation of the Practice Session

Evaluate the practice session as soon after its conclusion as possible. Indicate whether or not the performance objectives were achieved. Consider suggestions from your

"THE COACH GETS JAZZED EVEN WHEN WE HAVE A GOOD PRACTICE"

team, and ask your assistant coaches to give their input to this evaluation. In addition, include anything else you may have observed about the practice session that you think is important to record.

Principles for Designing Effective Practice Conditions

You may design and implement practice conditions in many different ways, but to be effective for proper learning they must be consistent with the following principles.

Principle 1. Practice the Skill in Contest-like Conditions as Soon as Athletes are Able to Do So

Structure your drills so that they simulate contest conditions. The more your drills are similar to the actual competitive situation, the more helpful they will be to playing the sport.

Practice the skill at the speed it is to be performed in competition, provided it can be executed safely and with a reasonable degree of accuracy. This produces more rapid and effective learning than does emphasizing slow, accurate movements and gradually increasing the speed. On the other hand, if the skill requires both speed and accuracy, equal emphasis should be placed on both during the practice session.

Principle 2. Practice Should Be Short and Frequent When Learning a New Skill

When athletes first learn a skill, they are likely to make many errors and tire quickly. Therefore, the skill should be practiced frequently, but not for too long. In other words, when youngsters must use considerable mental and physical effort to perform the skill, practicing the skill should be interspersed with either rest intervals or the practice of another skill that uses different muscle groups and demands less effort.

If you decide on rest intervals, you can use them to explain to the team what they need to do to improve their execution of the skill. If you use another skill instead of a rest interval, have the team practice the new skill for 10 minutes, another skill for 10 minutes, and then the new skill again for 10 minutes.

Sometimes it is beneficial to divide the team into small groups to practice new skills.

A modified version of this latter approach can be used in situations when all of the athletes cannot practice a certain skill at the same time. In such situations, divide the team into small groups and have them practice different skills at the same time. After a certain amount of time (e.g., 5 minutes), have each group practice another skill. Continue this routine until each group has practiced all of the skills planned for the session. When you use this approach, remember to consider the mental and physical effort required to perform each of the skills. If a group has just finished practicing a skill that demanded a great deal of effort, the next skill they practice should require less effort or different muscle groups.

When the athletes' skill level improves, you can increase the time devoted to practicing it. It is still a good idea, however, not to practice any one skill for too long. Ten or 15 minutes per drill is usually enough.

Principle 3. Each Athlete Should Be Working on Some Aspect of the Sport Throughout the Practice

Nothing is more boring for youngsters than to stand around for a long time and watch someone else perform. You can avoid this problem by using your practice time efficiently—which results from careful planning. Try to have each athlete working on some aspect of the sport during every moment of the practice.

Principle 4. Practice Conditions Should Make Maximum Use of Available Facilities and Equipment

Design your drills, practice formations, and so on to make efficient use of the facilities and equipment available. You can check your design efficiency by asking yourself two questions: First, is a facility or piece of equipment not being used that could be used? And second, could a facility or piece of equipment be used in a better way?

Principle 5. The Athletes Should Experience A Reasonable Amount of Success at Each Practice

If you have set realistic instructional goals, as discussed in chapter 8, and you have helped your athletes set realistic personal goals, as discussed in chapter 6, your athletes will be no strangers to success. One way to structure regular opportunities for success is to be certain that at each practice session the athletes engage in at least one skill or activity which they can perform reasonably well. You can also compliment as many members of the team as possible for correct performance of the whole skill or parts of it. And if some young athletes didn't perform anything correctly at a practice but made a sincere effort, praise them for that and encourage them to keep trying.

If the team is having difficulty performing a skill correctly, have them take a break or

practice some other aspect of the sport and come back to that skill later. It is sometimes better to back off from a new skill and approach it freshly later. Forcing the learning process is likely to produce failure and frustration.

Principle 6. Create a Practice Atmosphere in which the Athletes Are Not Afraid of Making Mistakes

We have already emphasized the importance of this principle in chapter 6. Remember, mistakes are a natural part of the learning process and should never be ridiculed by you, your assistant coaches, or the youngster's teammates or parents. Discourage anyone from making fun of or blaming an athlete who makes a mistake or cannot perform a skill.

Principle 7. Let Your Athletes Help in the Planning of Practices

As a cooperative style coach, you should permit your athletes to suggest what they'd like to work on in upcoming practices. If their suggestions are appropriate, use them. When youngsters share the planning of practices, they are likely to be more motivated and to find the practice more meaningful.

Principle 8. Frequently Emphasize That Practices are for Improving

This principle seems obvious, but athletes all too frequently come to practice without the intention of improving. If members of your team have this attitude, you must help them change it if they are to improve. They should understand that each time they come to practice three things can happen to their performance: (a) it can stay the same, (b) it can get better, or (c) it can get worse. If they want their performance to improve, they must come to practice with the intention of improving.

Principle 9. Allot Time for Practicing Skills Which Need Improvement

We have mentioned this principle several times before. You can help your athletes identify those skills which need more practice by recording their progress on each skill. Athletes sometimes spend too much time practicing what they already know how to do well because they can experience success—at the expense of practicing those skills they need to develop. You need to be aware of this tendency, yet give each athlete the responsibility to practice skills on which he or she needs to improve. This is consistent with the cooperative style of coaching which helps athletes become independent.

Principle 10. Make Practices Fun

Avoid repetitive and boring practice sessions. You can make practices fun by using a variety of drills and gimmicks, changing your practice schedule occasionally, being enthusiastic, letting the team help in the planning of the practice, and having the youngsters engage in some competition during the practice.

Checklist for Planning a Practice Session

1. Prepare the plan for the practice in advance by using the instructional schedule, input from athletes and assistant coaches, and results of previous practices.

   ____ Record date.

   ____ Write performance objectives.

   ____ Identify and check equipment needed for practice.

   ____ Prepare the time schedule.

      ____ Allot time for warm-up.

      ____ Allot time to practice previously taught skills.

      ____ Allot time to teach and practice a new skill.

      ____ Allot time to practice under contest-like conditions.

      ____ Allot time to bring the team together at the end of the practice for comments.

      ____ Allot time to evaluate the practice.

2. Meet with assistant coaches before the practice to go over the plan.

   ____ When?

   ____ Where?

3. Determine if the practice conditions are designed according to the following principles:

   ____ The skill is practiced in contest-like conditions as soon as athletes are capable of doing so.

   ____ Practice is frequent, but of short duration when first learning the skill.

   ____ Each athlete is working on some aspect of the sport throughout the practice.

   ____ Practice conditions make maximum use of available facilities and equipment.

____ The athletes experience a reasonable amount of success at each practice.

____ A practice atmosphere is created in which the athletes are not afraid of making mistakes.

____ Athletes help in the planning of the practice.

____ It is frequently emphasized to the athletes that they should come to practice with the intention of improving.

____ Athletes are allotted time to practice those skills which they need to practice.

____ Practices are fun.

CHAPTER 10

Teaching Sports Skills

It should be clear by now that to be the most effective coach you can be requires extensive planning. You have learned what you must plan for prior to the season, how to develop an instructional schedule for the entire season, and how to plan a single practice session. Now we will consider how to teach sports skills effectively.

One way to learn how to teach a skill is to observe Coach Befuddled. He will show you everything you should *not* do. He is unable to capture the attention of his athletes when he is ready to teach, probably because he cannot capture his own attention for more than 15 seconds at a time. When he speaks, it reminds you of Professor Gobbledygook—you can't understand half of what he is saying. His demonstrations usually confuse athletes more than help them because they are done poorly or incorrectly.

Coach Befuddled's lack of teaching skills frustrates his athletes because they learn little. Young athletes place great value on learning sports skills and they look to you, their coach, to help them learn. Thus, you should do all you can to become the best teacher possible.

Mastering the communication skills you read about in chapters 3 through 5 will be of great help to you in becoming a good teacher, as will be the planning you learned about in chapters 7 through 9. Although it also helps if you can perform the skills you will be teaching, being personally skilled in the sport is no guarantee that you have the skill to teach it properly. Some highly skilled athletes have a great deal of difficulty teaching the fundamental skills they learned many years ago. Remember, learning a skill is a skill in itself—just as much as any sport skill.

In this chapter, we discuss the four major steps in teaching a sport skill effectively:

Step 1
Introduce the Skill

Step 2
Demonstrate and Briefly Explain the Skill

Step 3
Have the Team Begin to Practice the Skill

Step 4
Provide Feedback to Correct Errors

Step 1
Introduce the Skill

Be enthusiastic in both your actions and your words when you introduce the skill. Avoid distractions such as sarcasm, annoying mannerisms, and abusive language. Speak clearly and use terminology your athletes can understand; the younger the athletes the simpler your words should be. Try to be brief, saying what you have to say in less than 3 minutes. Let's look more closely at the three events that make up this step.

Get the Team's Attention

Develop a regular routine for starting practice. Go to your usual place to begin practice and give a signal such as blowing a whistle to gain the athletes' attention. Position yourself so that you are facing the team when you speak to them. Make eye contact with the youngsters and say something like, "O.K., it's time to get started. May I have your attention please?" Speak firmly, politely, and slightly louder than normal conversational level. Once you have their attention, you should show your appreciation by saying, "Thank you."

If a few youngsters are inattentive, look directly at them, move closer to them and firmly but politely address them by name and ask them for their attention. If this fails, have them sit in another place where they cannot disrupt the practice session. Speak with these athletes either at an opportune time later during the practice session or at the end of it. When you are handling this problem, be certain to control your temper and keep your poise.

Arrange the Team
So All Can See and Hear

When you are speaking to your athletes, be sure to situate them in organized formations. If they are milling around or crowding together, it will be much harder for you to keep their attention. Shown in Figure 10.1 are good examples of team formation during discussions. Be certain with both of these formations that the background the

athletes see behind you is free of visual distractions and that the youngsters are not facing the sun. In addition, try to select a practice area with minimum noise so that they can hear you.

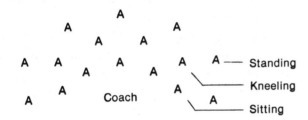

Figure 10.1—Team formations to use during demonstrations.

Name the Skill and If Appropriate, Give a Reason for Learning It

To name the skill simply say something like, "The basketball skill we are going to learn today is a two-handed chest pass." Sometimes, the reason for learning a particular skill is not always obvious to athletes, especially beginning athletes. For example, athletes may wonder why they need to learn to shoot a lay-up in basketball with their nondominant hand when they can already shoot it with their dominant hand. In this situation, it is advisable to briefly explain why.

Step 2
Demonstrate and
Briefly Explain the Skill

The skill should be demonstrated by someone who can perform the skill proficiently, and by someone whom the youngsters respect for being skilled in the sport. If

you are not certain about your ability to demonstrate a particular skill, either practice it until you can perform it effectively or get someone who can. Another alternative, if funds and equipment are available, is to use a film or videotape to demonstrate the skill. If none of these alternatives are possible and the demonstration cannot be given, you should seriously consider whether or not you should teach it. An effective demonstration consists of a sequence of four events, which we discuss next.

Prepare the Team for the Demonstration

To direct the team's attention toward the demonstration say something like, "Now that you are familiar with the skill, let's take a look at exactly how to perform it. May I have everyone's attention up here for the demonstration, please?"

Next, tell the team how you plan to give the demonstration and what to look for so that they will know what to expect. For example, you could say, "First I am going to show you what the skill looks like when it is performed in actual competition. I'll perform it several times, changing my position each time so that you all can get a good look at how the skill is executed."

Demonstrate and Explain the Skill

Whenever possible, demonstrate the whole skill just as it would be performed in an actual competitive situation. Demonstrate it for left-handers as well as right-handers. Demonstrate the skill several times so that the youngsters can see it performed from different angles. Before each demonstration, be certain to point out the important things to attend to during the demonstration.

If the skill is a complex one, you may have to demonstrate it again but at a slower speed. During this demonstration, direct the team's attention to the major sequence of actions that comprise the skill and to the most relevant cues that will enable them to perform the skill. Keep your explanation simple and brief. Be careful not to give them too much information.

Relate the Skill Being Demonstrated to Previously Learned Skills

After demonstrating the skill, the team should be made aware of any relationship between previously learned skills and the skill just demonstrated. You can do this by

---

Make the athletes aware of any relationship between previously learned skills and the new skill.

---

briefly explaining and demonstrating the similarities between the skills. For example, when a team is trying to learn the tennis serve for the first time and is having difficulty moving the arm holding the racquet through the proper sequence of movements, it is sometimes helpful to tell and show them how these movements are similar to a previously learned skill like throwing a ball. What you are doing is helping the team relate a skill that was previously learned (throwing a ball) to a new skill (tennis serve). This may help them learn at a faster rate.

Answer Relevant Questions About the Skill

After you have completed the first three events, ask the youngsters if they have

questions about how to perform the skill. When a child asks a question, repeat it so that everyone can hear. Answer only relevant questions and keep this event brief.

Step 3
Begin Practicing the Skill

Begin practicing the skill as soon as possible following the demonstration. Initially, you should try to get the athletes to make at least a gross approximation of the whole skill or part of it. To successfully complete this step, use the following three methods.

Arrange the Athletes and Show Them How to Practice the Skill

Use a formation that will allow the greatest number of athletes to safely and effectively practice the skill. The formation also should enable you to give them feedback about their performance. After you have put the youngsters in the desired formation, show them how the skill will be practiced. If a drill is used to practice the skill, be certain that it is easy to understand, simple to perform, and that it emphasizes the skill to be learned. Demonstrate how the skill is executed with a few of your best performers and be certain everyone knows how to proceed.

Motivate the Athletes to Practice the Skill

Young athletes usually find learning sports skills to be intrinsically motivating. When they do not, it usually is because they fear physical harm, fear failure, or aren't having any fun. If danger is an element in performing the skill, you must show the athletes how it has been minimized or eliminated. If athletes fear failure or aren't having fun, you should reread chapter 6 for suggestions on how to deal with this problem.

Practice the Skill

Once the team has begun practicing the skill, check to see that they are performing the drill properly. If they are not, stop them and make the necessary corrections. If they are, let them continue practicing it.

If most of your athletes are unable to perform the skill, stop the practice, and repeat the demonstration and explanation that you gave earlier. For some sports, you might want to take them through the skill slowly by having them perform the skill with you. To do this, simply face the same direction the team is facing and have them execute the skill with you slowly step-by-step. You may want to call out a key word or phrase for each of the movement steps as you begin to execute them. Check after each step to be certain that everyone is performing with you. Repeat this imitation procedure several times, answer any questions that may arise, and then have them begin practicing the skill.

age of the athletes on your team or teaching it incorrectly.

Sometimes, when athletes are unable to perform the whole skill, you can facilitate learning by dividing the skill into parts. Demonstrate and practice each part until the athletes can perform all of them reasonably well, then demonstrate and practice combining the parts until they eventually learn the whole skill.

Once the athletes are able to perform the whole skill well enough to practice it, look at the entire team for common performance errors which continue to reoccur. If you find one or more errors, stop the practice, present a brief explanation and demonstration of the error and its correction, answer any relevant questions, and then have them continue practicing the skill. After common errors have been corrected, begin working with individual athletes to help them refine their performance of the skill.

When working with athletes, coaches have a tendency to spend more time with the more gifted athletes or with those whom they like better than others, rather than spending it with those who need it. Try to avoid this, for it is one of the ways athletes decide whether you hold positive or negative expectancies of them.

When the team is practicing a skill, ensure they are performing it properly.

If your athletes still cannot perform the skill, don't persist, go on to something else. After practice, you can discuss the problem with some of your athletes and assistant coaches. They may be able to give you insight into why most of the athletes were unable to perform it. You may have been teaching a skill that was too complex for the

Step 4
Provide Feedback to Correct Errors

Practice alone is not enough to learn a skill correctly. For practice to be productive, it must be accompanied with feedback that provides athletes with information about their performance. Giving feedback so that it is effective in helping athletes correct performance errors involves three methods which are presented next.

"JUST A FEW COMMENTS ON YOUR PLAY TODAY SIMPSON..."

Observe and Evaluate Performance

Observe and evaluate the athlete's performance by comparing what he or she has done in relation to what should have been done. If you find an error, determine what is causing it as well as what advice can be offered to correct it. If you are uncertain about the cause of the error or how to correct it, give it more thought before making any suggestions. Continually giving incorrect or ineffective advice will diminish your credibility.

Sometimes you may observe an athlete making several errors. Because learning is more effective when an athlete attempts to correct one error at a time, you will have to decide which one you want to try to correct first. To do so, begin by determining whether or not one error is causing the other. If it is, have the athlete try to correct it first, because this will eliminate the other error(s). However, if the errors seem to be unrelated, have the athlete correct the error that you think will result in the greatest improvement. This improvement will likely motivate him or her to correct the other errors.

Give Feedback Effectively

Use the positive approach by complimenting effort and the parts of the skill that were performed correctly. Be sincere and honest with compliments. Do not indicate the effort was good or the skill was performed correctly when it was not. Athletes know when they have made a sincere effort or performed the skill correctly, and perceive undeserved praise for what it is.

Give simple and precise information about how performance can be improved. Tell as well as show the athlete what she or he has done as compared to what should have been done. Then do the same for what

"I THINK YOU PLANTED YOUR LEFT FOOT WRONG OR MAYBE YOUR RIGHT, WAIT THERE A SECOND AND WE'LL FIGURE IT OUT!"

must be done to correct the error. Be careful not to give too much information. Give just enough so that the athlete can concentrate on correcting one error at a time.

Make certain the athlete understands the feedback you presented. Simply ask the athlete to repeat what you said and did. If the athlete is unable to do so, be patient. Present the feedback again and ask the athlete to give it back to you.

Encourage the athlete to continue to practice and not to become discouraged if improvement does not occur immediately.

Provide Feedback As Soon After Performance and As Frequently As Possible

The sooner feedback is given the less likely athletes will forget what the feedback pertains to and the less likely the athlete will continue to practice incorrectly, making it more difficult to correct later. In addition, the more frequently athletes are given useful feedback, the more they will try to make the correction in their performance, and thus, the faster will be their learning.

In some situations, especially when athletes are a little older, you can have youngsters give feedback to each other. For example, to practice trapping skills in soccer you could arrange the athletes in groups of three. One athlete would perform the trapping skills, while another throws the ball to be trapped, and the third gives the feedback. After a certain time period or number of attempts to perform the skill, the players would change positions until each has experienced all three roles.

A word of caution, however: If youngsters are going to be used to give feedback, they must be told exactly what to look for when their teammates are performing the skill. They must also be told what the corrections are for common errors.

` JAMESON, WHEN ARE YOU GOING TO LEARN TO STOP TACKLING WITH YOUR HEAD.'

Teaching Evaluation Scale

This scale is designed to evaluate how you apply what you have read in this chapter. One way to use it is to sit down immediately after practice and fill it out yourself. Even better is to have another person who is familiar with the information in this chapter complete it after observing you teach a skill. Discuss the results with the person who evaluated you and use it as a guide to improve your teaching.

In the column at the left, indicate the most appropriate rating for each item as follows:

1 = Usually or always

2 = Occasionally or sometimes

3 = Seldom or never

4 = Not applicable for this practice

Step 1
Introducing The Skill

_____ Enthusiastic in actions and words.

_____ Avoids sarcasm, annoying mannerisms, and abusive language.

_____ Uses terminology the athletes can understand.

_____ Speaks clearly.

_____ Has a regular routine for starting practice.

_____ Faces the team when speaking to them.

_____ Makes good eye contact.

_____ Controls temper and displays poise when dealing with inattentive athletes.

_____ Uses a formation so the team can see the demonstration.

_____ Uses a formation so the team can hear the explanation.

_____ Identifies the skill to be taught.

_____ Introduces the skill in less than 3 minutes.

Step 2
Demonstrating and Explaining The Skill

_____ Directs the team's attention to the demonstration.

_____ Explains how the demonstration will proceed.

_____ Demonstrates the whole skill as it would be performed in competition.

_____ Demonstrates skillfully.

_____ Demonstrates for left-handers as well as right-handers.

_____ Demonstrates the skill several times.

_____ Demonstrates the skill so that it can be viewed from different angles.

_____ If necessary, demonstrates the skill at slower speed.

_____ Explains the major sequence of actions that comprise the skill when it is demonstrated at a slow speed.

_____ Points out the most relevant cues.

_____ Keeps explanation simple and brief.

_____ When appropriate, demonstrates parts of the skill.

_____ Briefly demonstrates and/or explains the similarities between skills.

_____ Repeats and answers relevant questions so all can hear.

Step 3
Practicing The Skill

_____ Begins practicing the skill as soon as possible after the demonstration.

_____ Uses a formation and drill that enables the greatest number of athletes to safely and effectively practice the skill.

_____ Uses drills which emphasize the skill to be explained.

_____ Demonstrates and explains how the drill works.

_____ Checks to be certain the team understands how the drill works.

_____ Eliminates or minimizes any danger involved in performing the skill.

_____ Creates an atmosphere in which fear of failure is minimized.

_____ Is in control of the team during practice.

_____ Checks to be certain all are proceeding through the drill correctly.

If the team is unable to perform the skill:

_____ Repeats the demonstration and explanation.

_____ If appropriate, takes them through the skill several times slowly and step-by-step and

_____ Uses "key" terms.

_____ Checks after each step to be sure that everyone is performing correctly.

_____ Repeats and answers relevant questions so all can hear.

_____ If the team is unable to perform the whole skill, has them master the parts.

When the team is able to perform the skill reasonably well:

_____ Stops practice and corrects common performance errors when necessary.

_____ When correcting common errors, presents a brief explanation and demonstration of the error and its corrections.

_____ Repeats and answers relevant questions so that all can hear.

Step 4
Providing Feedback
To Correct Errors

_____ Observes and evaluates performance.

_____ Compliments effort and parts of the skill that were performed correctly.

_____ Corrects one error at a time.

Gives simple and precise information:

_____ Tells and shows the athlete what he or she has done as compared to what should have been done.

_____ Tells and shows the athlete how to correct the error.

_____ Makes certain the athlete understands the information given.

_____ Shows patience with the athlete.

_____ Encourages the athlete to continue to practice and improve.

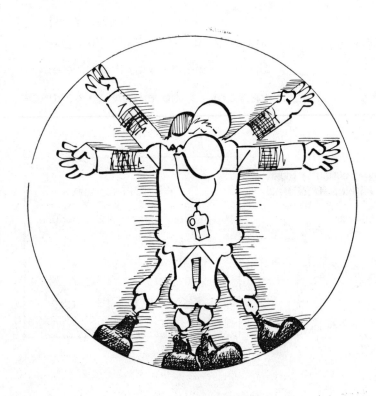

PART 4

Sport Physiology

CHAPTER 11
Principles of Training

CHAPTER 12
Developing Your Training Program

CHAPTER 13
Nutrition for Young Athletes

How do young athletes' bodies respond to exercise? How do the bodily systems adapt during well-planned training programs? The answers to these questions are the subject matter of Part 4.

How much should you know about this field? The dedicated coach never knows enough, never stops learning. You will not learn all there is to know in these next three chapters, but you can get started.

Today's young athletes want to know *why* they should practice twice a day, *why* they need to warm-up, *why* they are doing interval training, *why* they should not consume cokes and potato chips. You should be able to answer these questions. The three chapters in Part 4 will help you do so, and more importantly, will help you guide your athletes through a better training and nutritional program.

CHAPTER 11

Principles of Training

This chapter outlines physiological principles of training, principles that must be followed if your athletes are to make steady progress and avoid illness and injury. Read them carefully, keeping in mind the responsibility you accept when you become a coach. Remember that the human body is not fully matured until the late teens or early twenties, that the demands of growth require considerable energy and rest, and that sport should be developmental, not destructive.

Successful coaches understand and practice the following nine principles of training. Those who do not may ruin more athletes than they help.

Individual Response Principle

Athletes respond differently to the same training for some of the following reasons:

Heredity

Physique, ratio of fast and slow twitch muscle fibers (explained later), heart and lung size, and other factors are inherited. The well-endowed athlete may respond more favorably to training.

Maturity

More mature bodies can handle more training. Less mature athletes are using their energy for growth and development.

Nutrition

One coach took on the challenge of coaching a big city high school basketball team that had been a perennial cellar-dweller. He learned that these young athletes from the poor section of town often missed breakfast and might have soda pop and a chocolate cream cupcake for lunch. He instituted a nutrition program, taught defense, and was runner-up his first year. The next year his team won the league championship and he was named Coach of the Year. See chapter 12 to learn about nutrition, and you too may be Coach of the Year!

Rest and Sleep

Growing boys and girls need more rest, especially when they are involved in a vigorous training program. The coach can help by sending home recommendations re-

---

When involved in a vigorous training program, young athletes need more rest than normal.

---

garding a reasonable schedule for practice, studies, and sleep. The successful coach also knows when to suggest a day off from practice.

Level of Fitness

Improvement due to training is most dra-

matic when the level of fitness is low. Later, when fitness is high, long hours of effort are needed to achieve small changes.

Motivation

Athletes work harder and gain more when they are motivated, when they see the relationship of hard work to their personal goals. Young athletes who participate to satisfy their parent's goals are usually easy to spot. You need to counsel them so that they learn to set their own goals, even if that means not playing this sport.

Environmental Influences

Factors in the physical and psychological environment influence the response to training. When a youngster is under severe emotional stress at home or school, he or she does not need a coach adding to the burden. Heat, cold, altitude, and air pollution are factors in the physical environment that influence athletes' response to training. The coach must recognize this and suspend practice when the environment becomes too severe or a threat to health.

Disease or Injury

Of course, disease or injury will influence an athlete's response to training. The problem is to spot the disease or injury before it becomes serious. Many problems are first noticed during hard effort, so the coach may be the first to know.

In summary, successful coaches are aware of individual differences and how they affect the athlete's response to training. Successful coaches also are sensitive to changes in performance that may indicate poor nutrition, lack of rest, illness, or injury.

Adaptation Principle

Subtle changes take place in the body as it adapts to the added demands imposed by training. The adaptations include:

1. Improved heart function, circulation, and respiration;

2. Improved muscular endurance and strength; and

3. Tougher bones, tendons, ligaments, and connective tissue.

Ned Fredrick, a sport physiologist, has called training a gentle pastime in which we coax subtle changes from the body. The day-to-day changes are too subtle to measure. It takes weeks and months of patient progress to achieve success. Try to rush the process and you are asking for injury, illness, or both.

Overload Principle

The training program must place a demand on the body's systems for improvement to take place. As adaptation to increased loads occurs, more load should be added. The rate of improvement is related to three factors which you can remember by the acronym FIT.

- Frequency

- Intensity

- Time (duration)

The legendary tale of Milo, a warrior in ancient Greece, illustrates the Overload Principle. Milo started out lifting a young calf, and as the calf grew, so did Milo's strength. Eventually, he was able to lift the full-grown bull. Today, we use the Overload Principle in all kinds of training. We slowly add more weight to the barbell for strength training. Endurance athletes add more miles and hours of training. The overload stimulates changes in the muscles and other systems, changes designed to help the body cope with future demands. These changes involve the nervous system which learns to recruit more muscle fibers; the circulation which learns to distribute the blood to the muscles that need it; and the muscles themselves, where the overload stimulates the production of new protein to help meet the demands of future exercise.

LET'S SEE CHARLIE, AFTER SQUATS, WE'LL GO RIGHT TO SOME UPPER BODY WORK...

Progression Principle

To achieve adaptations using the Overload Principle, the training must follow the Progression Principle. When the training load is increased too quickly, the body cannot adapt; instead, it breaks down. Slow, steady progression must be observed in terms of:

Frequency
Sessions per week, per month, per year

Intensity
Training load per week, per month, per year

Time
Duration of training in hours per week, per month, per year

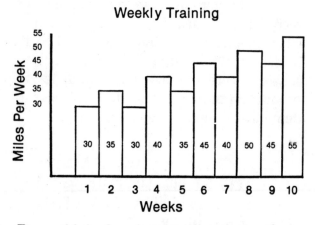

Figure 11.1 — Sample training progression chart.

In Figure 11.1 you can see the Progression Principle properly used for a young runner. Impatient coaches who have athletes progress too quickly at best cause athletes to peak too early and at worst to suffer injury or illness.

MAKE HASTE SLOWLY!

This principle also implies progression from:

The general . . . . .to the specific

The parts . . . . .to the whole

Quantity . . . . .to quality

In chapter 12, we will explain how to progress slowly in greater detail.

Specificity Principle

The type of training undertaken must relate to the desired results. Specific training brings specific results. For example, heavy weight training is of little value for the endurance athlete. Cycling is not the best preparation for running, or vice versa. Performance improves most when the training is specific to the activity.

Variation Principle

A training program must be varied to avoid boredom and achieve results. The Variation Principle embraces two basic concepts:

Work/Rest ... and ... Hard/Easy

Adaptation comes when work is followed by rest, when the hard is followed by the relatively easy. Failure to include variation leads to boredom, staleness, and poor performance.

Achieve variation by varying the training routine and drills. When possible, conduct workouts in different places. Follow a long workout with a short one, an intense session with a relaxed one, high speed with easy distance. When workouts become dull, do something different. Use variety to diminish monotony and lighten the psychological and physical burdens of heavy training.

Warm-up/Cool-down Principle

A warm-up must always precede strenuous activity (a) to increase body temperature, (b) to increase respiration and heart rate, and (c) to guard against muscle and tendon strains and ligament sprains (see chapter 14). A warm-up should consist of stretching, calisthenics, and gradually increasing exercise intensity.

" THAT WASN'T A BAD WARM-UP, NOW WE CAN START THE REAL WORKOUT ! "

The cool-down is just as important as the warm-up. Stopping an activity abruptly leads to pooling of blood and slow removal of waste products. It may also cause cramps, soreness, and more serious problems. Light activity and stretching continue the pumping action of muscles on veins, helping the circulation in the removal of wastes. The coach has the responsibility to teach the warm-up and cool-down and to include them in each training session.

Long-term Training Principle

Changes from the gradual overload of body systems lead to impressive improvements in performance. It takes years of effort to approach excellence, however. Long-term training allows for gradual progress, growth and development, acquisition of skills, learning of strategy, and a deeper understanding of the sport.

This does not mean an athlete needs to give up everything else to specialize in one sport. Young athletes should be encouraged to participate in a variety of activities. You should never expect or demand exclusive control over an athlete's free time. The need for specialization comes soon enough. Do not ask a young athlete to specialize in order to bolster your ego.

In time, as young athletes grow and develop, they will begin to spend more time on one or two sports. Those who want to reach the top must someday choose one sport and give it their undivided attention—for years. But don't rush the process; too much training too soon may lead to both mental and physical burnout. Excellence comes to those who pursue it with a long-term, non-pressured training program.

Reversibility Principle

Most of the adaptations achieved from hours of hard training are reversible. It takes three times as long to gain endurance as it does to lose it. With complete bed rest, fitness declines at the rate of nearly 10% per week. Strength declines more slowly, but lack of use will cause atrophy of even the best-trained muscles. The smart coach recognizes the Reversibility Principle and provides the team with off-season maintenance programs.

Checking Your Principles

You will want to remember the nine Principles of Training as you turn to chapter 12 and develop your own training program. Below is a simple matching exercise to check your memory. Match up the description in the right-hand column with the principle in the left-hand column.

Principle	Description
1. ____Individual Response	A. To avoid beginning and ending abruptly
2. ____Adaptation	B. Demanding more than usual from the body
3. ____Overload	C. Atrophy
4. ____Progression	D. Uniqueness
5. ____Specificity	E. Adjustment to overload
6. ____Variation	F. Years of effort
7. ____Warm-up/Cool-down	G. Reduce monotony
8. ____Long-term training	H. Training to meet the demand
9. ____Reversibility	I. Pacing the overload

Answers: 1=D; 2=E; 3=B; 4=I; 5=H; 6=G; 7=A; 8=F; 9=C

CHAPTER 12

Developing Your Training Program

Athletes must be fit to play well and avoid injury. Therefore, one of your major responsibilities is to help your athletes achieve the level of fitness demanded by the sport you coach. In this chapter, you will learn about two types of fitness—energy and muscular—and how to design a training program to help your athletes achieve each.

We will start with the warm-up, go on to energy and muscular fitness, then discuss the cool-down, and conclude with some observations about overtraining. That is a lot of territory to cover in one chapter, so we will not be able to tell you all there is to know—only enough to get started. We hope you find the topic so interesting that you will seek out additional information. To help you do so, we have listed additional reading material in Appendix A.

As you proceed, keep in mind how the athlete's age influences the purposes of training. In Figure 12.1, we show the stages of training according to age categories.

Warm-up

Each training session should begin with a warm-up designed specifically for your sport. When possible, begin on the mat, floor, or grass and have your athletes do slow stretching exercises for the low back, hamstrings (strong muscles on the back of the upper leg), and groin. Stretching increases range of motion, reduces risk of injury, and

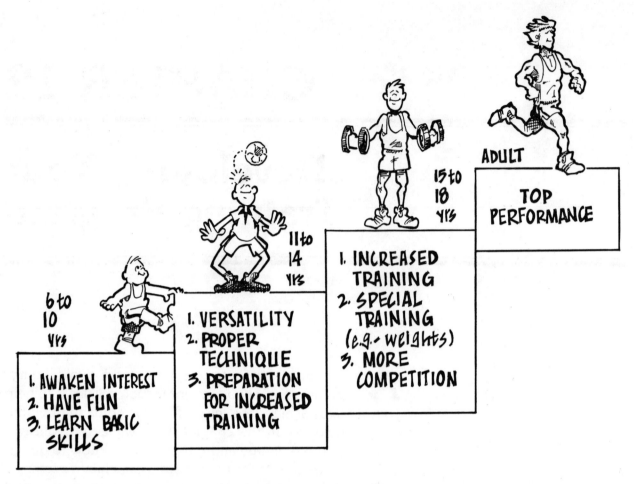

Figure 12.1—Stages of training.

relieves muscle soreness. Athletes should not try to stretch the muscles by "bouncing"; they should just reach until they feel discomfort or a slight, tingling pain. Then, have them hold for five counts and relax. Any muscles that get sore or are more easily injured when stiff should be stretched. Five minutes of stretching is usually adequate. Although you will want to use specific stretching exercises for your sport, a few stretching exercises that are helpful for most sports are shown here.

Next you can do calisthenics. Have your athletes begin with slow movements like push-ups and move to vigorous ones like jumping jacks in order to increase respiration, circulation, and body temperature. By now, the athletes are ready to practice skills. Do not begin scrimmaging, though, until they are completely warmed-up.

'DO YOU THINK WE MAY HAVE OVERDONE THE STRETCHING ROUTINE?'

WHILE STANDING, GRASP TOE OF FLEXED LEG AND FIRMLY PULL TOWARDS YOUR BODY TO STRETCH LEG. REPEAT A COUPLE OF TIMES & SWITCH LEGS ....

PULL KNEES TO CHEST & ROCK BACK & FORTH ON YOUR BACK.

WITH ARMS OUT-STRETCHED, KEEP-ING EYES FORWARD, TWIST TRUNK FROM SIDE TO SIDE...

IN HURDLERS POSITION SLOWLY STRETCH OUT & TOUCH RIGHT TOE WITH BOTH HANDS ~ SWITCH POSITION WITH LEFT LEG FORWARD & REPEAT. PERFORM ON EACH LEG SEVERAL TIMES.

USE JUMPING JACKS IN YOUR WARM UPS TOO ...

SIT WITH LEGS OUTSTRETCHED & SLOWLY STRETCH TO TOUCH YOUR TOES - REPEAT SEVERAL TIMES.

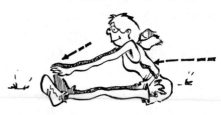

SLOWLY SLIDE INTO STRIDE POSITION WITH FRONT FOOT FLAT ON FLOOR AND REAR FOOT ON TOES. CHANGE EVERY 5 SECONDS.

STAND 3 FEET FROM WALL WITH HEELS ON GROUND, LEAN FORWARD SLOWLY, HOLD FOR 15 TO 20 SECONDS...

Energy Fitness

Energy fitness is the ability to store and use the body's fuel efficiently when participating in physical activity. As a coach, you should know how to help athletes achieve energy fitness. To do so, you must understand how the muscles use the energy available to them. This is important, as you will see, because the demands of different sports cause the muscles to use the energy differently. By properly training athletes, you can help them prepare their bodies to meet these differing demands.

Energy Pathways

The energy muscles use to contract comes from two sources or pathways. One pathway is called *aerobic* (meaning with oxygen) and the second is called *anaerobic* (meaning without oxygen). Which pathway

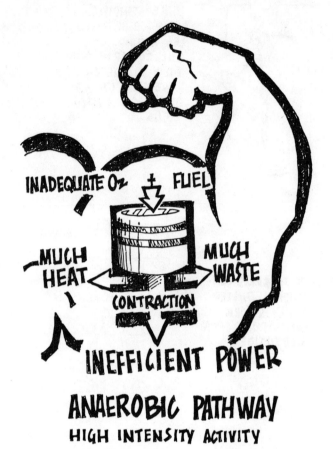

ANAEROBIC PATHWAY
HIGH INTENSITY ACTIVITY

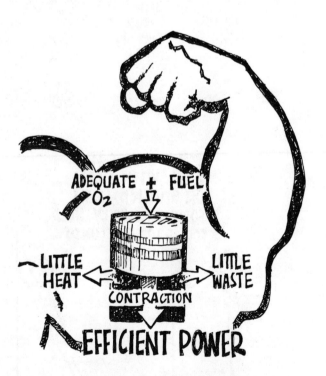

AEROBIC PATHWAY
LOW INTENSITY ACTIVITY

your body uses depends on the intensity of the activity.

Walking and easy jogging are examples of aerobic exercise, with the energy coming from the oxidation of fat and carbohydrate. But when the activity becomes very intense and the body can't supply enough oxygen to the muscles, some of the energy for muscular contractions comes from the anaerobic or nonoxidative breakdown of carbohydrate.

Fueling the muscle anaerobically is far less efficient than using the aerobic pathway. For example, when sugar is burned aerobically it produces 39 units of energy; when it is burned anaerobically it only produces 3 units. Furthermore, the inefficient anaerobic pathway produces a chemical called lactic acid which hinders performance.

In short, when athletes exercise at a level of intensity where enough oxygen is not available to the muscles, they are accumulating an *oxygen debt.* At some point, they must cease the activity and pay back the debt by permitting the body to adequately re-oxygenate the muscles. Fortunately, the body can be trained to run much more efficiently, and thus accumulate a smaller debt when exercising intensely. How athletes best train for energy fitness is the next topic of discussion.

Energy Training

It may be helpful for you to think of energy training as the building of a pyramid, such as the one shown in Figure 12.2. The training pyramid is built on an aerobic foundation.

Aerobic Foundation. Aerobic fitness, the ability to take in, transport, and utilize oxygen, is necessary for athletes in all sports. Aerobic fitness helps athletes avoid injuries and provides the toughness and endurance needed for more intense training. It prepares the aerobic foundation, the base upon which future practices and performances are built. Even in football, where the average play lasts but a few seconds, aerobic fitness

helps athletes recover faster between plays and allows more effective practice before fatigue sets in. Good aerobic training consists of:

- low intensity, long duration activity (e.g., distance swimming, bicycling, or running)
- natural intervals (long, easy distances with occasional short bursts of speed)
- hills or resistance work once a week

As endurance grows, you can increase the aerobic training by higher intensity and/or longer duration activity. Remember, the intensity should not be so great that the muscles use the anaerobic energy pathway. It is far more efficient to use oxygen, so get all you can from the aerobic pathway before you move on to more intense anaerobic training. Follow the principles of training outlined in chapter 11. Start slowly, use progression, overload the system with distance and then intensity. Use variety to keep training interesting. Follow hard with easy, work with rest.

Finally, you should recognize that intense aerobic training is not as effective for young athletes, so hold back on long, hard training until the youngsters reach puberty. You may help them avoid the early "burn out" that often accompanies excessive training.

Anaerobic training. Anaerobic energy pathways are best trained when they are overloaded in short, intense exercise bouts. Anaerobic training is achieved through progressive increases in speed with decreases in distance. This method of training, called interval training, involves an exercise interval followed by a period of *active rest,* such as easy jogging.

We provide some basic interval training suggestions in Table 12.1. Study this table carefully; it is a useful guide for designing your anaerobic training program.

Identify the intervals in Table 12.1 which most closely approximate the activity in

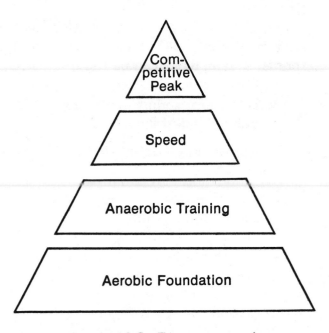

Figure 12.2—Training pyramid.

Table 12.1

Interval Training Suggestions

Intervals	Repetitions	Duration of each Repetition	Exercise/ Rest Ratio*	% of Maximum Speed	% of Maximum Heart Rate
Long	4-6	2-5 min	1:1	70-80	90
Medium	8-12	60-90 sec	1:2	80-90	95
Short	15-20	30-60 sec	1:3	95	100
Sprint	25+	10-30 sec	1:3	100	100

*1:1 means the rest lasts as long as the exercise interval.
 1:3 means the rest is 3 times as long as the exercise interval.

your sport. According to the principle of specificity discussed in chapter 11, you should train your athletes using these intervals. Follow closely the guidelines given in the columns, "% of maximum speed" and "% of maximum heart rate." Maximum heart rate is commonly computed by the following formula:

Maximum heart rate = 220 − Age in years

To avoid overworking young or less fit athletes, be sure the heart rate recovers

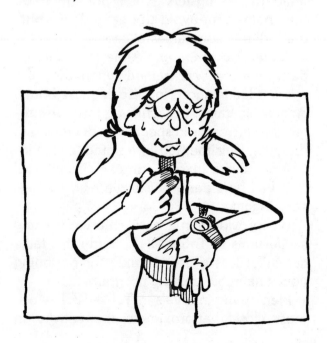

below 125 beats per minute before the next interval begins. When young athletes are no longer able to maintain good form, the interval training should be stopped. Never schedule more than two high intensity workouts per week. A game or competition counts as a high intensity workout.

Anaerobic training takes no more than 6 weeks. Therefore, start the higher intensity training 6 weeks before you want the athletes to be in top form. Too much anaerobic training leads to staleness, illness, and injuries.

Speed. Now the athlete is ready for speed work if it is needed. For sports that require sprints, several types can be used:

- acceleration sprints—start easy then speed up (safest kind)

- hollow sprints—fast at start and finish, easier in middle

- starts—if needed for such sports as track, swimming, football

For skill sports like basketball, the best speed work is on the court (line drills), using the ball (fast break drills).

Competitive peak. In Figure 12.3, you can see how these forms of training fit into

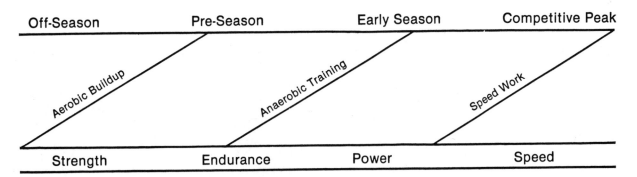

Off-Season	Pre-Season	Early Season	Competitive Peak

Aerobic Buildup   Anaerobic Training   Speed Work

Strength	Endurance	Power	Speed

Figure 12.3—Year-round training program.

an overall training program. Focus your attention on the time frame for each type of training. We will explain how the training for strength, endurance, power, and speed are tied into this time frame shortly.

Aerobic training can be accomplished in the off season. Doing so will enable athletes to begin anaerobic training when they report for preseason practice. If they are not prepared, you must take the time to develop the aerobic foundation.

As practice progresses, so does the intensity of training. You should not attempt to achieve peak performances in the early season. Use early games or meets to sharpen skills, and do necessary speed work to bring the team to a peak as the season progresses. By midseason, the athletes should be at a competitive peak that can be maintained for the rest of the season. If athletes peak too soon, the team may slump before the season ends.

Muscular Fitness

Muscular fitness includes strength, endurance, power, and speed. In Figure 12.3, you can see how these components of athletic performance can be woven into the training program, starting with strength, then endurance, power, and finally speed. We will give you some help in training athletes for each component of muscular fitness.

Strength

The first question you should answer is: How much strength is required in the sport? If the sport demands more strength than the athletes have, then strength training is needed. If, however, athletes don't need additional strength training, move on to endurance, power, or speed work.

Strength training for prepubertal athletes does little good. Moreover, attempts to lift heavy weights could cause injuries in youngsters whose bones are still forming. Do not encourage younger athletes to lift heavy weights, and be sure the older athletes follow the guidelines listed in Table 12.2.

Strength improves when the muscle is overloaded. A weight that can only be lifted a few times is sufficient to overload the muscle and cause adaptation. Gradual progression using free weights, weight machines, or

Table 12.2

Strength Training Guidelines

1. Do serious strength training in the off season.

2. Use lighter weights for the first few days to avoid soreness.

3. Exhale during the lift, inhale when lowering the weight.

4. Always work with a spotter when lifting free weights (barbells).

5. Alternate muscle groups during a workout.

6. Keep accurate records of progress (weight, repetitions, maximum strength, body weight, muscle girth, etc.).

7. As with all other forms of training, select exercises specific to the sport.

calisthenics will improve strength when you follow this basic prescription.

1. Set the amount of weight so the maximum number of repetitions is 6-8. Increase the load when the athlete can do more than 8 repetitions.

2. Do 3 sets of lifts for each muscle group.

3. Lift 3 times per week.

Calisthenics are another way to build strength if you can resist the movement (e.g., as with push-ups) and keep the repetitions under eight. If the athletes can do more than 8 or 10 repetitions, they will be building endurance instead of strength.

Some calisthenics like the chin-up are self-limiting; you can only do so many. Others like the push-up need added resistance, such as a partner's hand on the back to build strength. Work in pairs using the newest technique of strength development—variable resistance training. With this method, the athlete does a push-up, for ex-

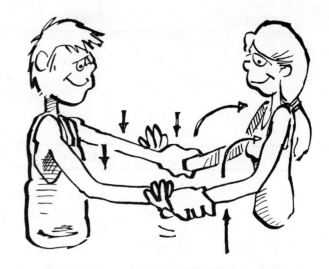

RESISTANCE TRAINING

ample, against the resistance (counterforce) provided by a partner. The resistance is varied to match the force of the contraction. For best results, athletes should go through the movement in 1 to 2 seconds. With a little imagination, you can devise other "counterforce" exercises.

Follow the strength program 3 times per week and your athletes will improve at the rate of 1 to 3% per week. When they have achieved an adequate level of strength for the sport, stop the strength training and move on to other things. Occasional strength work should be done during the season to be sure the strength is not lost.

How do you know which sport demands more strength or if certain athletes need more? In some cases, it is obvious. Football players, especially interior linemen, need lots of strength, distance runners do not. Strength is defined as the maximum amount that can be lifted *one time*. Many sports, such as swimming, basketball, and cross-country skiing, involve the repetitions of less than maximum (submaximal) contractions, and that takes more endurance than strength. Athletes can use more strength if the load or resistance encountered in the sport is greater than 20% of their maximum strength.

"I THINK SOME STRENGTH TRAINING MAY BE THE TICKET HERE..."

The benefits of strength training depend on the individual athlete, in accord with our Individual Response Principle in chapter 11. One of the factors determining how individuals respond to strength training is the proportion of slow and fast twitch muscle fibers they have inherited. Humans have two main types of muscle fibers—slow and fast. The slow fibers are not strong but have considerable endurance. The fast fibers are more powerful but tend to fatigue quickly. Athletes with more slow fibers make good endurance athletes; those with more fast fibers are better suited for fast sports such as sprints and jumping.

Although the proportion of each fiber type is inherited, both can be improved through specific strength or endurance training. For prepubertal athletes, however, do not waste your time or theirs on strength training. They may need endurance training, however, so read on.

Muscular Endurance

When swimmers need only 20% of their strength to pull their arms through the water, they do not need more strength; they need the energy and endurance to continue exerting that 20% throughout the race. Follow these procedures to develop muscular endurance in your athletes:

1. Use more than 10 repetitions, the actual number and resistance depending on the sport for which you are training.

2. Use many repetitions and little resistance for long duration sports and fewer repetitions and more resistance for shorter events.

3. Do 3 sets of lifts for each muscle group.

4. Lift 3 times per week.

Like strength training, endurance exercises should be specific to the way the muscles will be used in the sport. When possible, try to imitate the movement as it is used in competition. Use weights, weight machines, calisthenics, or other methods to achieve results.

Endurance is extremely trainable. Improvements in the muscle's energy pathways and its use of fat and oxygen can increase endurance greatly. In time, athletes can go from 20 to over 200 push-ups or more! Often, the dramatic improvement in endurance leads to athletic success.

Power

Power is the *rate* of doing work which can be described as:

$$\frac{Force \times Distance}{Time}$$

As such, it involves the components of strength (force) and speed (distance divided by time). It is an essential ingredient in such sports as football and ice hockey. Training for power differs from strength training in that strength training is usually done rather slowly, whereas power training is done as fast as possible. To train for power, have athletes practice the movement as fast as they can, using resistance equaling 30-60% of their maximum strength.

Barbells are not well-suited for this type of training. Weight machines are somewhat better, but the best approach is to use modern variable resistance devices that allow control of the resistance *and* speed of contraction. With these devices, you can dial the resistance and speed you need and safely conduct the program. Another plus with this type of training is that muscles do not get sore as easily. Soreness is caused by letting down the weight or an overly vigorous effort in the early season.

"BEST WAY I'VE FOUND TO TRAIN FOR SPEED."

Speed

You may have heard that sprinters are born, not made. This is essentially true, because fast muscle fibers are inherited. All athletes, however, can use specific speed training to improve reaction and movement time. (Reaction time is the time needed to decide to make the movement. Movement time is the time from the start of a specific movement to the end of the movement.)

Fast reactions are taught in practice drills. The smart coach does so by narrowing the choices athletes must make to just a few. Movement time also can be enhanced by power training, which may help speed up a resisted movement (e.g., shot put, football block). Movements with a small resistance can be enhanced with specific speed training. For example, have the athletes run down a slight grade to increase running speed. The secret to speed training is to do a movement faster than it is normally done, and in some cases, as fast as possible.

Cool-down

Be sure your athletes have a chance to cool down after a vigorous practice session. Light activity such as jogging, walking, and stretching helps the circulation clear metabolic by-products from muscles, reducing the likelihood of stiffness and soreness. It may look good to follow wind sprints with a spirited dash to the shower room, but it is not the best thing for the athletes.

Overtraining

As coach, it is your job to conduct an effective training program. When doing so, remember the Principles of Training: *Train don't strain.* Overtraining is far worse than undertraining. The former leads to injury or illness, the latter only delays attainment of

Table 12.3

Energy Needs and Training Programs for Popular Sports

Sport	Energy Needs	Training Emphasis*
Baseball, football, ice hockey	Short, intense efforts (under 10 seconds)	Anaerobic training and speed
Basketball, soccer, tennis, wrestling, lacrosse, gymnastics	Intense, but longer efforts (under 2 minutes)	Anaerobic training
Certain swimming and track events, skating	Middle distance or duration events (2 to 10 minutes)	Aerobic training Anaerobic training
Cross country running and skiing	Long distance events (over 10 minutes)	Aerobic training

*Be sure to develop the aerobic foundation before you begin higher intensity training.

the competitive peak. Be alert to the signs of overtraining:

- chronic fatigue

- irritability

- decreased interest

- weight loss

- reduced speed, strength, and endurance

- slower reflexes

- poor performance in sport, school, or work

When you suspect overtraining or impending illness, talk to the athlete. If you develop a good, honest relationship with your players, they will not hesitate to tell you when they feel run down. Lighten their training load or give them the day off.

Finally, in Table 12.3, we have grouped the more popular sports according to the energy needs of the sport and then indicated which training program(s) is appropriate. If your sport is not shown, find one that is similar in energy needs to determine the appropriate training emphasis.

Key Points to Remember

1. Each training session should begin with a warm-up designed specifically for your sport.

2. Muscles depend on two major sources of energy: carbohydrate and fat. Carbohydrate is the most efficient fuel for the muscles.

3. The two major pathways which provide energy for muscles are aerobic and anaerobic. The aerobic pathway is very efficient; the anaerobic is far less efficient.

4. The energy pathway used depends on the intensity of effort:
   A. Fat and carbohydrates are burned during low intensity.
   B. Carbohydrates are burned exclusively as intensity increases.

5. Training should begin with slow, easy distance training to develop the aerobic foundation.

6. When training becomes intense, it improves the anaerobic energy pathways.

7. Muscular fitness consists of flexibility,

strength, endurance, speed, and power.

8. Strength improves when the muscle is overloaded. The coach must determine how much strength is needed for the particular sport.

9. Muscle endurance is extremely trainable by doing low resistance, high repetition exercise.

10. Power or the rate of doing work combines the strength (force) and speed with which a movement is made.

11. Strength training is usually done slowly; power training is done as fast as possible.

12. Speed can be trained by practicing the movement faster than it is normally done.

13. The "cool-down" through light activity and stretching is important after a vigorous practice or contest.

14. Coaches should be alert to signs of overtraining.

CHAPTER 13

Nutrition for Young Athletes

Most coaches recognize the importance of good nutrition for their athletes but find it difficult to implement a sound nutrition program. First, junk foods are so popular, it is hard to keep young people from eating them. Second, helping athletes eat right requires the cooperation of parents, who are responsible for preparing the food. And third, there are many myths about nutrition and sport—e.g., the use of vitamin supplements, high protein diets, and salt intake to name a few—so athletes and coaches may be misinformed.

In chapter 13, we will introduce you to the basics of good nutrition for athletes. You will learn about the foods that are highest in energy, the need for vitamins and minerals, the pregame meal, losing and gaining weight, and the high performance diet.

Energy

Young athletes will find it hard to train and perform if their diet lacks energy. The typical growing youngster needs about 2500 calories of energy a day. Athletes who burn over 500 calories in a vigorous training session need additional calories. Thus, young athletes' total daily energy needs can exceed 3000 calories.

Most Americans eat more fat and protein than they need. For athletic performance and good health, we recommend a diet which emphasizes carbohydrates —what we call the *high performance diet*. In Table 13.1, you can readily compare the typical diet with the high performance diet.

Table 13.1

Comparison of the Percent of Calories in the Typical Diet With the High Performance and Health Diet

	Typical diet (%)	High performance diet (%)
Fat	40	20
Protein	15	15
Carbohydrate	45	65

Fat

Athletes do not need much fat in their diet; 10% is probably enough. But fat does enhance the taste of food and helps fill us. Athletes' fat intake should be reduced not only for health reasons, but because it does not help athletic performance. Also, too much fat in the precompetition meal can cause nausea.

Protein

Notice that in Table 13.1 the protein level is 15% for both the typical and the high performance diet. Although we stated that most Americans get more protein than they need, we left the protein level the same because active bodies need protein for the additional growth and development stimulated by training, as well as for tissue repair. Young boys and girls need about 50-60 grams of protein daily, and more if they are

involved in heavy training. With maturity, protein needs go down; most adults can get by with 10% of their calories from good quality protein.

Quality protein contains a good supply of the nine essential amino acids, protein building blocks that cannot be manufactured in the body. Although animal protein is better supplied with these essentials, meat is not the only or the best source for protein, as is commonly thought. The best bet is to eat a variety of the foods listed in Table 13.2.

Incidentally, protein only serves as a source of energy when a person is on a starvation diet. Athletes who diet heavily to lose weight must be warned that they lose tissue protein in the process. This loss could weaken the athlete and hurt performance. Moreover, hard training while dieting could adversely affect growth during a critical period. (We'll have more about weight loss later in this chapter.)

Carbohydrate

You may be surprised to see carbohydrate as the leading source of energy in the high performance diet. Carbohydrate is the major source of energy throughout the world. Some underdeveloped countries get as much as 80% of their calories from carbohydrate, and they suffer far less heart disease.

Natural carbohydrate such as potatoes, corn, beans, rice, and whole-grained products are nutritious and healthy. Concentrated or refined carbohydrate, such as table sugar, is a poor source of energy for it is packed with empty calories. Furthermore, eating concentrated sugars stimulates a large outpouring of the hormone insulin, which hurries the sugar out of the blood. This causes the blood sugar level to become too low—a condition called hypoglycemia—which leaves athletes feeling nonenergetic. Corn, rice, and other com-

Table 13.2
Some High Protein Foods

Food	Measure	Protein (grams)
Bacon	3 strips	8.0
Beans		
• and pork	1/2 cup	8.0
• lima	1/2 cup	6.0
• red	1/2 cup	8.0
• soy	1/2 cup	10.0
Beef		
• corned	3 slices	21.5
• roast	2 slices	24.0
• steak	1/4 pound	25.0
Biscuits	3	7.0
Cheese		
• American	1 ounce	7.5
• cottage	1/4 cup	7.5
• Swiss	1 ounce	8.5
Chicken	3 1/2 ounces	25.0
Chili with beans	1 cup	19.0
Clams	1/2 cup	8.0
Crabmeat	5/8 cup	17.5
Egg	1 large	6.5
Fish	4 ounces	25.0
Flour		
• white	1 cup	11.5
• whole grain	1 cup	16.5
Ham	3 1/2 ounces	21.0
Lamb	3 1/2 ounces	22.0
Lentils	1/2 cup	8.0
Lobster	2/3 cup meat	18.5
Macaroni and cheese	1 cup	19.0
Milk	1 cup	10.0
Peas		
• split	1/2 cup	10.0
Pork		
• chop	1	15.0
• loin	2 slices	20.0
Pizza	1/6 of 14 inch	12.0

plex carbohydrates are slow to enter the blood stream, thus keeping insulin levels steady. This increases the amount of carbohydrates used as an energy source and reduces the amount stored as fat.

Incidentally, honey is a natural but concentrated source of sugar that is similar to table sugar in how it's absorbed into the body. It has only small amounts of essential nutrients. Fresh fruits, on the other hand, are another source of sugar and are highly nutritious.

High Performance Diet

So the best diet for the athlete, regardless of age, is a low-fat, high-carbohydrate diet. Vigorous activity draws energy from carbohydrate stored in the muscles (muscle glycogen). The high carbohydrate diet refills the muscles so they are ready to go the next day. Athletes who eat a low carbohydrate diet won't be able to keep going during a hard practice because they won't have enough muscle glycogen.

As discussed in chapter 12, fat and carbohydrate are burned during activity, but during intense effort, the body turns to muscle glycogen. If muscles lack glycogen, they cannot sustain vigorous contractions in practice or competition.

REALLY INTO HEALTH FOOD, EH SHAKLEY?

Table 13.3

Daily Food Plan

Food group	Value in diet	Recommended daily intake
Milk group (milk, cheese, cottage cheese)	Protein, calcium, other minerals, and vitamins	3 or more servings (preferably low fat)
Meat group (also includes fish, fowl, nuts, peas, beans)	Protein, iron, other minerals, and B vitamins	2 or more servings (consider more fish and beans, and less meat)
Vegetables and fruits (includes potatoes)	Minerals, vitamins, and fiber	4 or more servings
Breads and cereals (include rice and pasta)	Carbohydrate energy, protein, iron, and B vitamins, fiber	4 or more servings

Balanced Diet

Good nutrition means eating a variety of foods from the four basic food groups. Diets that concentrate on one food or exclude a group are likely to spell trouble. Most athletes can more than adequately meet their nutritional needs by eating a balanced diet with special emphasis on carbohydrates. A good daily food plan can be developed from Table 13.3.

Nutrients

In addition to a small amount of fat, essential proteins, and enough energy to fuel a full day's effort, the young athlete needs vitamins and minerals to help regulate the chemistry of the body. Coaches and athletes have often been told that certain vitamins and mineral supplements will help athletes perform better. You will find that this is seldom true as you learn more about the nutrients young athletes need.

"I'M TELLIN YA HAROLD, THERE'S NO SUCH THING AS A VITAMIN C WITHDRAWAL!"

Vitamins

Vitamins come in two general categories: fat soluble (A, D, E) and water soluble (B, C). The difference between fat soluble and water soluble vitamins is that unused portions of fat soluble vitamins are stored in the body's fat, whereas water soluble vitamins are washed away in the urine. Vitamins help cause chemical reactions in the body to produce energy. Thus, vitamins are essential because they help convert the food we eat into energy. When athletes don't have enough vitamins, they are unable to get enough energy. But this does not mean huge doses of vitamins will provide extra energy. As stated previously, excessive doses of vitamins B and C are eliminated in the urine, and extra amounts of A, D, and E can be stored, sometimes with unhappy results. Toxic levels of vitamin D affect calcium levels and could retard an athlete's growth. So if a little bit is good, more is not necessarily better.

Athletes need more vitamins as they use more energy, but eating more will usually take care of this need. Only youngsters who are extremely active or those in weight loss programs (which must be carefully supervised) should take a daily vitamin supplement to be sure their vitamin needs are met. Vitamin supplements will not benefit the health or performance of athletes already on an adequate diet.

Minerals

Calcium, phosphorus, magnesium, iodine, zinc, and iron are some of the minerals considered essential for good nutrition. Iron is particularly important to young athletes, both male and female. Much of the iron absorbed into the blood goes into the production of hemoglobin in the red blood cells. The iron in hemoglobin helps carry oxygen from the lungs to the working muscles. If youngsters don't have enough iron in their diet, they will become anemic, which will dramatically affect their athletic performance.

Only about 10-20% of the iron in the diet is absorbed into the body, so young athletes must take in 10 times the amount they need daily. Athletes from low-income families are more likely to be iron deficient, perhaps because they eat less high-cost meats which are rich in iron. Dates, prunes, apricots, raisins, and most beans, however, contain iron. If you are concerned about an athlete's iron intake, suggest a daily vitamin with iron, along with a diet that draws from a variety of iron-rich foods.

Zinc is another mineral receiving substantial attention among athletes in recent years. Zinc is needed for growth, blood cell formation, and tissue repair. Athletes should not waste their money on expensive zinc supplements; they can obtain an ample supply of zinc simply by eating whole-grain foods.

Pregame Meal

Much too much has been made of the pregame meal. It isn't a big deal. In fact, if an athlete is on the high performance diet, a typical meal would probably be quite adequate. The major thing about the pregame meal is it must be easily digested and out of the stomach before competition. Athletes should eat at least 3 hours before the contest and avoid large quantities of fat. They should eat enough to feel satisfied but not stuffed. Nervous athletes may do better with a liquid meal.

It's no more necessary to eat tea and toast than it is to consume a steak before competition. A pregame meal is like driving your car down the street to do an errand: A half tank of gas is plenty; the car won't run better on a full tank, and neither will your athletes.

Athletes participating in distance events such as running, cycling, swimming, and cross country skiing sometimes prefer not to eat on the day of competition. A high carbohydrate meal before long distance competition is not good because muscle glycogen is used too fast, hastening fatigue. Dur-

I TAKE IT PANCAKES ARE YOUR
FAVORITE PRE-GAME MEAL EH STINSON?

ing a long distance event, fluid with a small amount of sugar (25 grams per liter) can be helpful. High sugar concentrations slow the passage of sugar and water into the blood. In very long events (over 3 hours), when the pace is slower, athletes can and should take more sugar.

Gaining and Losing Weight

Weight gain or loss is a matter of energy balance. If athletes eat more calories than they burn, they'll gain weight; if they burn more than they eat, they'll lose weight. It's that simple.

Ideal Weight

Is there an ideal weight for athletes? Yes, but it depends on the sport, the athlete's body build, age, and sex. The ideal weight for athletes is most easily determined by finding out how much of their weight is fat and how much is lean mass (muscles,

bones, and vital organs). It's important to remember when determining ideal weight that girls have a naturally higher percent fat than boys.

In some sports like distance running, athletes do better when the percent body fat is low (5% for boys and 12% for girls). In other sports, such as basketball, the percent body fat is not as important, although athletes in any sport do not want to be carrying excess weight. Well-conditioned athletes average about 8-12% fat for boys and 16-22% for girls. The percent body fat should never go below 4-5% for boys and 10-12% for girls. The body needs a certain amount of fat to insulate nerves, protect vital organs, and help in the metabolic process.

To help athletes achieve their ideal weight you need some means to determine accurately their body fat. Several procedures for doing this are available; the most practical is measuring the fat just under the skin using a device called skinfold calipers. About 50% of the body's fat is stored beneath the skin, and knowing this helps us readily predict the body's total percent of fat.

Although the skinfold method is a relatively simple idea, applying it requires skill and more knowledge. Learning to use skinfold calipers is beyond the scope of this book, but is something you should learn as you obtain more sports science and medicine education. Learning to take skinfold measures and calculate the percent body fat is beyond the scope of this introductory text.[1]

Without these more precise procedures, you must rely on your good judgment as to whether athletes need to gain or lose weight. The ideal weight is the one that feels good and allows athletes to perform well. If

---

[1]If you want to learn how, read *Coaches' Guide to Nutrition and Weight Control* by Patricia Eisenman and Dennis Johnson. Available from Human Kinetics Publishers, Box 5076, Champaign, IL 61820.

weight or fat go too low, the athlete will become weak and listless. When weight is too high, it interferes with performance and could become a health problem. Now let's consider how to gain and lose weight.

Weight Gain

For many of us gaining weight is easy—too easy. But for some young athletes interested in sports like football, weight gain can be difficult. Here are some guidelines you can use to help your athletes gain weight.

1. Increase the calories consumed by 2500 for each pound of lean tissue to be gained.

2. Increased caloric consumption should be combined with a strength training program to gain muscle rather than fat weight.

3. Weight gain should be slow and gradual, increasing caloric intake by no more than 1000 calories per day over daily needs.

4. Avoid eating extremely large meals; instead eat more often.

5. Consume the largest portion of the caloric intake early in the day.

6. Avoid excessive amounts of animal fats and salty foods.

7. Do not permit athletes to use drugs such as androgenic hormones or anabolic steroids to promote weight gain.

Gaining weight so that an athlete is at his or her ideal weight is healthy. But remember that excess weight, be it fat or muscle, is bad for the health. Extra muscle or fat often means higher blood pressure, and that means a higher risk of heart disease. *Any coach who encourages or allows athletes to gain extra bulk has the responsibility to help*

those athletes return to a healthy body weight after the season. This responsibility means a postseason weight loss program that emphasizes calorie-burning exercises, like running. As a coach and teacher, you cannot shirk this responsibility.

> Gaining weight so that an athlete is at his or her ideal weight is healthy.

Weight Loss

Although gaining weight takes effort, even more difficult is losing weight. The three major approaches to weight loss are:

- exercise
- diet (caloric restriction)
- behavior modification

Exercise. The best way to lose weight is by exercising; it burns off more fat and conserves muscle protein. Diet leads to a greater loss of protein and water and a smaller fat loss. Moderate exercises like running, cycling, swimming, hiking, and cross country skiing are good ways to burn off 10 or more calories per minute. Other sports like tennis, which burn 7 to 8 calories per minute, also are good because they can be continued for several hours.

Diet. One good way to avoid excess weight is to avoid the extra calories in the first place. Skip the giant burger, fries, and shake and you avoid the need to burn off 1300 calories (13 miles of running). The weight loss diet does not mean more or less of some basic food, just fewer calories in general—and less junk food. When weight loss is combined with vigorous training, a vitamin supplement may be helpful.

Exercise and diet together will speed

weight loss. The caloric deficit (the difference between what you eat and what you burn), however, should not regularly exceed 1000 calories per day. For example, if an athlete burns 3000 calories and eats 2500, the deficit is 500. Over a 7-day period, the deficit would be 3500 calories, which is equivalent to a 1-pound weight loss.

If the athlete increases his or her exercise by 500 calories per day, the deficit would be 1000 calories per day. In 7 days, a 7000 calorie deficit would result in 2 pounds of weight loss. So weight loss should never exceed 2 pounds per week. Athletes who lose weight faster than this rate will find it very difficult to engage in practice or competition.

Behavior modification. Eating is behavior that needs modifying. Overweight athletes should eat only at mealtime and only at the dining room table. They must learn to put less on their plate and eat only one serving. Breaking bad eating habits requires the same type of discipline that is necessary to become a skilled athlete. Help your athletes discipline themselves—and be a good example!

Dehydration

The body has an elaborate system designed to maintain the best fluid balance in tissues, body fluids, and the blood. Disrupting the system may have serious, sometimes life-threatening, consequences. Even moderate dehydration will have a noticeable effect on performance, because not only does dehydration rid the body of necessary water, but it also alters the balance of electrolytes. Electrolytes are charged molecules of sodium and potassium—minerals which are located in the fluid inside and outside of cells. Dehydration draws the electrolytes which are inside the cells to the fluid outside, affecting nerve conduction and muscle contraction, and ultimately, decreasing

athletes' strength. Also, athletes' endurance drops due to inadequate blood volume. When wrestlers or boxers dehydrate to "make weight," they risk diminished strength and endurance, and more.

Water weighs about 2 pounds per quart. It is easy to sweat off 3 or 4 quarts (6 to 8 pounds) during a hot practice. Water loss in excess of 2 to 3% of body weight can affect performance. Greater than 5% dehydration causes marked decline in performance and risks heat exhaustion. When combined with a starvation diet, dehydration can have serious health consequences.

Avoid the need to dehydrate. Help athletes select a target weight early in the season and achieve that weight gradually. Remember that young athletes are growing; they need energy, essential nutrients, and water. Deprive them and you could affect their growth and their health. No sport is that important!

Playing in Hot Climates

When exercising in a hot climate, the body is usually able to maintain a safe temperature with the evaporation of sweat.

It is not the sweating but the evaporation of sweat which cools the body. Thus, if sweat drips off the body, it doesn't have time to evaporate, and the body loses only water, not heat.

A young athlete can lose as much as 2 quarts of sweat each hour of practice or competition. This water must be replaced or the body becomes dehydrated, and the dehydrated body does not function well. Water level can be maintained in most sports by: (a) drinking 1-2 cups of water before practice or competition, (b) taking frequent drinks during the activity, and (c) continuing to drink after the game. (The body's thirst mechanism always underestimates its fluid needs.)

Although sodium or salt is lost in the sweat, the loss is not as much as you might think. Because most young athletes get plenty of salt, supplementing salt intake usually is not necessary. By using the salt shaker at mealtime, athletes will more than adequately replace the lost salt.

Potassium may be depleted after many days of work in a hot climate. This can easily be replaced by eating citrus fruits and drinks, potatoes, bananas, and other potassium-rich foods.

Some coaches like to use "athletic drinks" that contain salt, potassium, and some sugar. These are fine but unnecessary if you provide plenty of water and schedule practices and games in the cooler parts of the day.

When you anticipate competing in hot climates, you can prepare your athletes in several ways

1. *Fitness.* Aerobic fitness enhances the circulatory system, which is responsible for heat transfer. Also, fit individuals start to sweat sooner and do not get so hot.

2. *Acclimation.* Four to 8 days of practice in the heat will prepare young athletes to compete in the uncomfortable environment.

3. *Clothing.* Select uniforms and equipment that allow sweat to evaporate.

4. *Instruction.* Make sure athletes know how important it is to drink lots of water, encourage them to salt their food during the hot days, and make sure they eat potassium-rich foods.

" COACH, WHAT DID YOU CALL THIS DRINK AGAIN?"

Key Points to Remember

1. Young athletes may need 3000 or more calories per day to meet their energy needs.

2. The high performance diet for best athletic performance and good health is 65% carbohydrate, 20% fat, and 15% protein.

3. Good nutrition occurs when athletes select a variety of foods from the four basic food groups, with special emphasis on carbohydrates.

4. Vitamins are essential because they

help convert food into energy. A well-balanced diet provides all the vitamins and minerals an athlete needs.

5. The pregame meal is no big deal. Athletes should eat a well-balanced meal, high in carbohydrate and low in fat, at least 3 hours before competition.

6. Weight gain or loss is simply a matter of energy balance. If athletes eat more calories than they burn, they'll gain weight; if they burn more than they eat, they'll lose weight.

7. Increased caloric consumption in order to gain weight should be gradual and combined with a strength training program.

8. Weight loss is best achieved by a combination of exercise and caloric restriction.

This will require athletes to learn to modify their eating behavior.

9. Depriving athletes of water in order to lose weight or during intense physical activity is foolish, for it risks heat exhaustion and damage to vital organs.

10. Drink plenty of water—the best liquid—when exercising in hot climates.

11. Athletes do not need salt tablets to replace lost sodium unless the salt loss is extraordinarily great.

12. At altitudes above 5000 feet encourage a high carbohydrate intake. As oxygen becomes less available, the body relies on carbohydrates for energy during exercise.

PART 5

Sports Medicine

CHAPTER 14
Injury Prevention

CHAPTER 15
First Aid for Athletic Injuries

CHAPTER 16
Rehabilitation of Sports Injuries

Who usually attends to the injured athlete first? Who usually is the person to administer first aid before a player sees a physician? Who can *prevent* a large number of these injuries with a good injury prevention program? If you haven't already guessed, it's the coach.

Of the several million athletic injuries that occur yearly, approximately 80% are initially seen and given first aid by the coach. Unfortunately, less than half of these coaches have had any athletic first aid training. The purpose of Part 5, "Sports Medicine," is to help you prevent athletic injuries, and to deal with them effectively when they occur.

CHAPTER 14

Injury Prevention

Injury prevention is the most important aspect of sports medicine. The old adage "an ounce of prevention is worth a pound of cure" is especially true with athletic injuries. A carefully planned and executed injury prevention program will keep your athletes off the "injured list" and on the field.

As with skilled sports performances, injury prevention does not just happen—you have to make it happen! It begins with careful preseason planning of conditioning, coaching techniques, and equipment. You can often find clues as to how injuries occur by reviewing the injuries of the previous season. For example, you may find that several sprained ankles were caused by an uneven practice field.

An effective injury prevention program requires daily attention and supervision. You will need to make sure that equipment fits and is being worn properly, that techniques are being taught properly, and that the rules of play are being followed.

Is it worth it? Of course it is! Every year, several million athletes are injured in sports; a few even die. As coach, you are in a position to help stop this epidemic of injuries. Injury prevention works—make it work for you!

Preparticipation Examination

Before youngsters participate in sports, they must be in good health. Therefore, each youngster should have a medical examination before the season starts. The exact nature of this examination will vary depending on the age of the athlete and the sport involved. The yearly examination most youngsters receive will be enough for many sports; be sure to also require a simple note from the athlete's physician stating that he or she is healthy. For other sports, a specific preparticipation examination may be required with special forms and parental permission slips. The exact type of examination athletes need is best decided by your youth sport organization with appropriate consultation from physicians.

Collect the examination slips with the completed Player Information Form, discussed on page 69. If your team travels, you *must* have parental permission for care of the child in case of emergency. Doctors cannot treat an injured child without parental permission. An Emergency Medical Treatment form, such as the following sample, could be duplicated on the back of the Player Information Form—and it should travel with the team.

Athletes who are ill should not be certified to play in a sport until they are cleared by their physician. Minor colds may not be a reason to withhold an athlete, but fever, vomiting, diarrhea, muscle aches, or other serious illnesses should be. Allowing sick athletes to play may well prolong their illness or even make it worse.

Handicapped children may be certified to participate through a mutual decision of parents, athlete, physician, and coach. All should understand the youngster's limitations as well as any additional risks to which he or she may be exposed. Although the risks involved with a handicap may prevent a youngster from participating in a particular sport, it does not mean they are to be excluded from all sports. For example, a deaf child would be at additional risk in a contact sport such as football, but would do well in various noncontact sports such as tennis or track and field.

Physical Conditioning

We have already emphasized the importance of conditioning your athletes for the demands of your sport (see chapter 12). Failing to do so can lead to many minor injuries, such as muscle strains, and to major injuries, such as broken bones. Major injuries are more likely to occur when athletes become tired while playing.

A note about conditioning: Although athletes may be in shape for one sport, they may need to "recondition" themselves for another sport which requires the use of different skills or muscle groups (e.g., swimming vs. soccer or tennis vs. basketball).

Emergency Medical Treatment Form

We, the parents of _____,
give permission for emergency medical treatment of our child for illness or accident if we cannot first be contacted.

Date _____ Parent or Guardian _____

Emergency Phone:

_____ Parent or Guardian _____

_____

Matching
Athletes for Sports

Athletes should be grouped according to their size and physical maturation rather than their age. Some sports like wrestling do this in part with weight categories, but other sports like football or basketball may overlook these differences. Two 13-year-old boys, for example, may be amazingly different in size and physical maturation. One boy may be thin, 5'5", and weigh 100 pounds. He may have no hair under his arms and no facial hair. The other boy may be muscular, 5'11", and 160 pounds, with both facial and body hair. If these two athletes collide, the smaller athlete could be seriously hurt.

When youngsters of the same age or age group are obviously mismatched in physical maturation or skill level, your organization should be flexible enough to permit youngsters to be placed in leagues more appropriate to their size and ability. Programs which put winning first and athletes second do not offer such flexibility. As a result, the less skilled, less mature athletes are at greater risk.

Another question which has created much controversy in youth sports is whether girls should be allowed to compete with boys. The answer is—it depends. It depends on the sport and maturity of the boys and girls. Prior to puberty, boys' and girls' strength and muscle mass are hardly different. They can compete on an equal basis at this age in all sports.

At puberty, boys begin to make rapid gains in strength, muscle mass, and body weight. This puts girls at a definite disadvantage and at risk of injury in contact and collision sports. We recommend that after puberty, girls and boys do not participate together in contact (baseball or basketball) or collision (football or hockey) sports. Mixed participation in endurance and non-contact sports is encouraged, however. In fact, it is now becoming apparent that girls not only can offer good competition, but may top their male counterparts in many of these sports.

Because it is difficult to predict exactly when puberty occurs, it may be best to draw the line between elementary school and junior high school-age children. Therefore, after starting junior high, girls and boys should not participate together in contact or collision sports.

Protective Equipment

Many sports, such as football, baseball, and soccer, require various pieces of protective equipment to help prevent injury. This equipment must be in good condition and checked before it is given to the athletes. Do not use "hand-me-down" equipment unless it is in good repair and properly reconditioned. Be aware of any safety standards that have been set for the equipment you

issue (e.g., the National Operating Committee for Standards in Athletic Equipment), and make sure your equipment meets or surpasses these standards.

Be certain that the equipment is properly fitted to each athlete. The best equipment in the world does little good if not fitted well. If you do not know how to fit the equipment, contact other coaches or trainers at the college or professional level who do know. Athletes should be taught how to maintain their equipment and use it properly. Problems with equipment should be reported to the coach immediately. During the season, make periodic checks to see that equipment is in good repair.

Finally, remember that the field or court is part of the equipment. Therefore, it also should be in good repair—free of holes, glass, protruding sprinkler systems, and obstacles like trees or walls.

stand how to use it. Be sure to take any necessary safety precautions, such as using spotters or mats. Do not allow athletes to use equipment or apparatus like the parallel bars or vaulting horse without supervision!

As we said earlier, it is natural for youngsters to "horse around." However, this behavior often results in a large number of injuries. Athletes need to understand that self-discipline can easily prevent these unnecessary injuries. Horseplay with equipment or on an apparatus must not be tolerated.

Rules in many sports are there to prevent injuries; make sure your athletes understand and abide by them. Remember, most athletic injuries occur in practice, so this is not a time to overlook the rules of a sport. Athletes who break rules in practice will also break them in competition.

Proper Supervision

Properly teaching and supervising skills will help prevent many injuries. Not only is it expected when you assume the role of coach, but as discussed in chapter 17, you have a legal responsibility to do so.

Sports skills should be taught in the proper sequence, which we discussed in chapter 8. If a piece of apparatus is involved, make sure you and your athletes under-

Warm-up and Flexibility

Although we have already discussed the warm-up and how to do it properly, we want to reinforce its importance for preventing injuries. Warm-up exercises need to be performed not only before practices or games, but also when athletes are coming off the bench and entering the game and at the beginning of the second half of a competitive event.

Heat Injury

Heat illness (heatstroke, exhaustion, or fatigue) is a potentially serious problem and is totally preventable. If you work your athletes hard in a hot, humid environment and do not replace their fluid losses from sweating with adequate water breaks, the athletes may become seriously ill. As the body loses fluid, its cooling mechanism starts to fail and body temperature climbs. When this continues, the body finally overheats and the athlete goes into shock, and even may die.

An adequate injury prevention program will eliminate those factors causing heat injury. Working your athletes hard in a hot environment with sweat suits and no water does not make them tough—it may make them dead!

Factors that predispose athletes to heat injury during practice or games are: (a) a hot day, (b) humidity, (c) clothes that prevent proper evaporation of sweat, (football uniforms, sweat suits—"barrier clothing"), (d) no water breaks, and (e) taking salt tablets. You can decrease these risk factors by doing the following:

1. Schedule practice during the cooler parts of the day (early morning or evening).

2. Cancel practice on excessively hot and/or humid days.

3. For football, where many heat injuries occur, have players work out without pads or in t-shirts and shorts. Use "net type" jerseys. Have them take their helmets off when not engaged in contact activities. No sweat suits on hot days!

4. Schedule and enforce water breaks at regular times. Many recent studies have shown time and time again that the best fluid is water.

5. Salt tablets are taboo! Athletes do not drink enough water to dilute them and the extra salt may be toxic.

1. HOT DAYS
+ 2. HIGH HUMIDITY
+ 3. BARRIER CLOTHING
+ 4. SALT TABLETS
+ 5. NO WATER
= R.I.P. YOUNG ATHLETE

Injury Prevention Checklist

Below is a list of questions to consider prior to, during, and after the season to help prevent injuries among your athletes.

Preseason

_____ Have the athletes had a medical examination?

_____ Are the athletes properly matched for sex, size, and skill level?

_____ Have the athletes undergone adequate preseason conditioning?

_____ Are the equipment and facilities in good repair?

_____ Have you prepared warm-up drills?

_____ Can you properly teach the skills?

Season

_____ Is your training program satisfactory?

____ Are athletes using the protective equipment properly?

____ Do your athletes know and abide by the rules of the sport?

____ Do you adequately supervise your athletes to eliminate horseplay and improper use of equipment?

____ Do you take the proper action to prevent heat injury?

Postseason

____ Did you evaluate your training program to determine if it was satisfactory?

____ Did you evaluate your ability to teach skills properly?

____ Did you examine the equipment and apparatus?

____ Did you review the injuries that occurred this past season?

CHAPTER 15

First Aid for Athletic Injuries

We hope your injury prevention program will also prevent you from using the skills presented in this chapter. During the year, however, you will undoubtedly see some injuries. About 2/3 will occur during practice and you will be the person responsible for first aid. A coach rarely has a fully equipped ambulance with medics or a certified athletic trainer available during practices—and seldom so during contests.

The purpose of this chapter, therefore, is to provide you with the skills necessary to care for injured athletes until they can be seen by a trainer and/or physician. Some of these skills require only simple, common-sense procedures, whereas others are more complex, such as the life-saving cardiopulmonary resuscitation (CPR) procedure. You need to know the first aid procedures in this chapter well and be able to use them quickly if the need arises.

Preseason Preparation

It is important to have a well thought-out "game plan" for dealing with injuries. Do you have a first aid kit? Do you know where the nearest phone is and how to get an ambulance? Do any of the other coaches know first aid? Who will go for help if you are needed to attend the injured player? The middle of an emergency is no time to realize you do not know who or how to call for help!

Here are the things you should do before the season begins:

1. Buy a first aid kit if you don't have one.

2. Obtain the telephone numbers for the emergency services in your community and put them in your first aid kit.

3. Be sure you know this chapter well and learn more if you can. (See the reading list in Appendix A.)

4. Discuss your emergency plan with your assistant coaches and your athletes so everyone knows what to do.

Transporting The Injured Athlete

Transporting injured athletes may not present much of a problem; they may be running around, howling, and holding a stepped-on finger. Athletes with more serious injuries, however, or with minor injuries of the lower extremities may need some assistance in getting to a medical facility. If you are in doubt about the seriousness of the injury or how to transport the athlete correctly, WAIT for professional medical help to arrive.

Unstable fractures and especially head, neck, and back injuries require special training and equipment for proper transport. DO NOT move an athlete with a serious head injury or suspected neck or back injury! Improper transport can result in a more serious injury—perhaps permanent paralysis.

Do not move an athlete with a fracture unless you have splinted it first. Again, if you're unsure about how to do this, wait for qualified help.

If an athlete has a minor injury to a lower limb, he or she can usually be carried or helped by teammates under your direction. Be sure the help you recruit is strong enough for the job.

Never allow your athletes to attend to injured players or help them up unless you have instructed them to do so. Injured players are your responsibility, not the athletes.' Make sure everyone on the team understands this!

Cuts, Scrapes, and Bruises

Cuts, scrapes, and bruises are everyday occurrences in many sports. Most are obviously minor and can be treated with simple first aid. The objectives in treating these minor injuries are to:

1. Stop the bleeding;

2. Cleanse the wound thoroughly; and

3. Protect the wound.

Stop the Bleeding

Cuts and some scrapes may bleed freely. Cuts around the head are often prone to profuse bleeding. Also, athletes with an injured artery can lose a large amount of blood. Arterial bleeding can be recognized by the spurting or pumping of blood from the wound. The proper technique to stop bleeding is to apply *direct pressure* to the wound by firmly holding a clean dressing against it. If you are unable to stop the bleeding with direct pressure, seek medical assistance immediately. A tourniquet is rarely necessary to control serious bleeding of an arm or leg. Apply the tourniquet above the wound if attempts to control bleeding with direct pressure fail.

CLEANSE THE WOUND

soapy water. After you have scrubbed the wound and are sure all the dirt and other foreign matter are out of the wound, gently rinse the injury with clean water and pat dry with a clean towel or sterile gauze. Unless all the dirt is worked out of the wound, infection may result—so be thorough.

DIRECT PRESSURE

To stop the bleeding from a tongue that has been bitten, gently hold a clean dressing on the cut. Keep the athlete sitting up so that he or she doesn't choke on the blood or swallow excessive amounts.

Proper Cleansing

Once the bleeding has been controlled, the wound needs to be cleaned to prevent infection. The most important part of cleansing a wound is to use adequate rinsing with a forceful stream of clean water or a good scrubbing with a clean cloth and mild,

Protect the Wound

Once cleansed, the wound needs to be protected from dirt and further injury. If the wound has been cleansed well, it is not necessary to apply any type of first aid cream;

DRESS WOUND WITH CLEAN GAUZE & ADHESIVE TAPE.

however, you may do so if you wish. A sterile gauze or band-aid should be used to cover the wound. A wound that has edges gaping open may need stitches or bandages. If the athlete continues to participate, the wounded area should be protected with gauze or some sort of protective padding.

A clean dressing should be applied daily to a wound. At that time, the wound should be checked for any signs of infection, such as an increase in pus, pain, and a spreading red area around the wound. If the infection is significant, you should seek medical assistance.

The Bloody Nose

A bloody nose often can be a tough problem. The correct way to stop the bleeding is to have the athlete sit down and firmly pinch his or her nostrils shut for several minutes. Alternately, a small tampon (such as a feminine hygiene tampon) can be inserted into the bleeding nostril to provide direct pressure to the bleeding area and removed 15-20 minutes later. If these methods fail, you must seek medical assistance.

Strains and Sprains

Athletic competition often results in injury to muscles, tendons, or ligaments. A *strain* is an injury to a muscle or tendon; a *sprain* is an injury to a ligament. When athletes sprain an ankle, they have injured the ligaments. When athletes pull a hamstring, they have strained the muscle or tendon.

These injuries merely may be a minor overstretching or a partial or complete tear in the structure. Generally, the more severe the injury, the more pain and disability the athlete experiences. Most of these injuries require careful evaluation by an athletic trainer or physician to determine their extent. Proper first aid, however, at the time of the injury can greatly reduce the discomfort and speed the athlete's return to play.

The first goal of treating a strain or sprain is to limit the swelling in the hours following the injury. The muscle or joint is not recovered until all the swelling is gone. If you can limit this swelling by proper first aid, the athlete will return to play more quickly. And that proper first aid is the immediate application of *ice*.

Heat or hot water has no place in first aid of strains or sprains! Heat increases the blood flow to the injured area and results in an increase in swelling! *Heat is not neat!*

To help you remember the proper sequence of first aid for athletic injuries, just remember the word ICE:

- Ice
- Compression
- Elevation

Ice

Ice is one of the most important parts of an athletic first aid kit. Regular cube ice or crushed ice can be placed in plastic bags and easily stored for ready use in a small, styrofoam cooler. (Commercially prepared ice packs are not as good as plain ice and are an unnecessary expense.) The bag of ice should be placed over a couple layers of an elastic bandage and wrapped over the injury. Wet the elastic bandage to allow it to better transmit the cold to the injury. Alternately, the ice bag may be placed directly on the skin.

Compression

Compress the injured area by gently wrapping the ice bag in place with the remainder of the elastic bandage. The wrapping should be gentle and firm but not tight. If the elastic bandage is wrapped too tightly, you may cut off circulation to the underlying skin which, because of the ice, could produce frostbite.

Elevation

Elevate the injury after the ice and elastic wrap have been applied. The injured limb should be propped up so that it rests higher than the heart. This allows any fluid that is collecting to drain away.

After providing first aid, have an athletic trainer or doctor see the athlete to evaluate the injury. The sooner the athlete is seen, the better the doctor can examine the injury. If you wait until the following day, the injury may be so tender that the athlete cannot stand the pain of a careful examination. Friday's injuries should not be seen on Monday!

Ice, compression, and elevation also are good first aid for large bruises, especially on large muscles.

First Aid of the Sprained Ankle

The sprained ankle is one of the commonest injuries in sports. The four steps to treating this injury are:

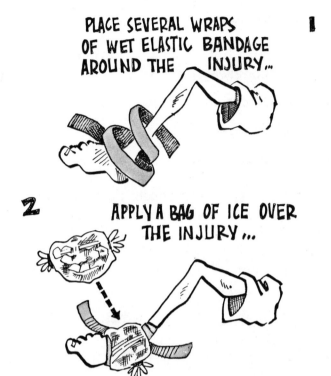

PLACE SEVERAL WRAPS OF WET ELASTIC BANDAGE AROUND THE INJURY... **1**

2 APPLY A BAG OF ICE OVER THE INJURY...

WRAP THE ICE BAG IN PLACE **3** WITH THE REMAINDER OF THE ELASTIC BANDAGE...

4

ELEVATE THE INJURED LIMB.

Heat Injury

Heat injury is a life-threatening condition! If one of the athletes collapses after exertion in a hot environment, you must act quickly. Symptoms the athlete may exhibit prior to collapse are:

- Dry, hot skin with no sweating (not always)
- Confusion
- Dizziness
- Chills on the chest

If you see or an athlete describes any of these symptoms, you must cool him or her immediately. *If the athlete is conscious:*

1. Remove any headgear and other heavy clothing.
2. Douse with cold water, ice, or ice towels;
3. Give cool liquids by mouth;
4. If improvement is not quick—GET HELP.

If the athlete is unconscious:

1. Remove clothes;
2. Cool by packing body with ice, cold towels, or douse with cold water.
3. Do not give liquids by mouth;
4. Call an ambulance;
5. Give CPR if athlete stops breathing.

The Unconscious Player

Being knocked unconscious is a serious injury and requires immediate medical assistance. First aid should be limited to making sure that the athlete is breathing and that his or her mouth and throat are clear of turf, blood, or vomit. If the mouth and throat are not clear, clear them out with your finger. Administer CPR if the athlete stops breathing.

Be careful about moving the athlete; besides having a concussion, he or she may also have a neck injury. When the athlete becomes conscious, keep him or her quiet and in place until seen by a trainer or doctor.

Cardiopulmonary Resuscitation (CPR)

This small section on CPR is not a substitute for a Red Cross- or American Heart Association-sponsored course on CPR. We urge you to take one of these courses now offered in most communities. This section will introduce you to the essentials of CPR or perhaps serve as a refresher to those of you who have already taken a course.

CPR can be life-saving and must be administered as soon as it is established that an athlete has stopped breathing. It must be continued uninterrupted until the ambulance arrives. Do not give up, for some people have been saved after prolonged CPR. CPR is as simple as ABC:

- Airway
- Breathing
- Cardiac

This is how you should remember the technique. As soon as you know the victim has stopped breathing, you must act.

Airway

Clear the athlete's airway (mouth, nose,

and throat) of blood, vomit, or debris. Use your fingers and do this step quickly. Second, position the athlete on his or her back and open the throat by gently tilting the head back so that the chin protrudes upward. A rolled-up towel or jacket placed under the neck is helpful in maintaining this position.

AIRWAY

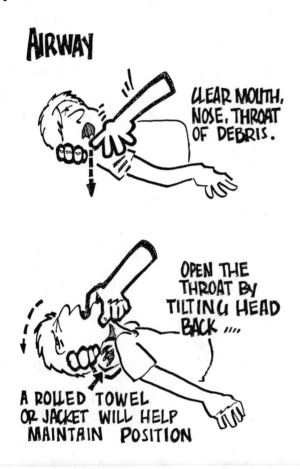

CLEAR MOUTH, NOSE, THROAT OF DEBRIS.

OPEN THE THROAT BY TILTING HEAD BACK ....

A ROLLED TOWEL OR JACKET WILL HELP MAINTAIN POSITION

Breathing

Place your mouth over the athlete's mouth (or mouth and nose with smaller people) and deliver short, forceful breaths. If you cover only the athlete's mouth with your mouth, it is important to pinch the nostrils closed so air does not escape but goes to the lungs. The athlete's chest should rise upward with these breaths, which should be delivered at a rate of around 15 per minute. In the 4 seconds between breaths, 4-5 cardiac compressions should be delivered.

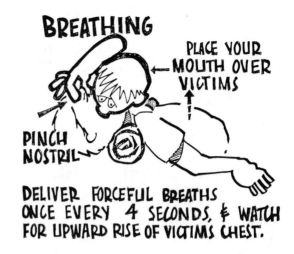

BREATHING

PLACE YOUR MOUTH OVER VICTIMS

PINCH NOSTRIL

DELIVER FORCEFUL BREATHS ONCE EVERY 4 SECONDS, & WATCH FOR UPWARD RISE OF VICTIMS CHEST.

Cardiac

If you are unable to locate a strong pulse or heartbeat, the athlete will require cardiac compression. This should be performed in conjunction with the breathing so that every 4 to 5 compressions are interspersed with a breath: 1-2-3-4-5-BREATH-1-2-3-4-5-BREATH-1-2-3-4-5-BREATH.

The compressions should be produced by quickly and forcefully depressing the athlete's breastbone or sternum using both hands placed over the middle of the chest. The compressions are to be delivered rapidly, so that 4-5 compressions take no more than 4-5 seconds.

Although the entire resuscitation can be

CARDIAC

SHOULD BE PERFORMED IF UNABLE TO LOCATE STRONG HEARTBEAT

... USE IN CONJUNCTION WITH BREATHING.

.... COMPRESS 1,2,3,4,5, BREATH - REPEAT

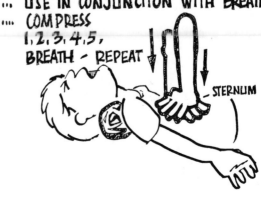

STERNUM

performed by one person, it is best to have one rescuer breathe for the athlete while the second rescuer delivers the cardiac compression in a coordinated manner with the breathing. Finally, obtain medical assistance immediately!

Athletic First Aid Kit

From what you have learned in this chapter, you should know what to place in your athletic first aid kit. Check to see that you have at least the following:

____ Ice, ice chest, and plastic bags

____ Elastic bandages

____ Soap

____ Bandages and gauze

____ Band-aids

____ Splint material

____ Clean water

____ Athletic tape

Key Points to Remember

1. Have a "game plan" so you know who to call, how to call, and what to do in case of serious injury.

2. Remember to bring the first aid kit with emergency telephone numbers to practice as well as games (2/3 of the injuries occur in practice).

3. The essentials of wound care are:

   a. Stop the bleeding

   b. Cleanse the wound

   c. Protect the wound

4. Remember and practice the ABCs of ICE.

5. Know and practice CPR.

CHAPTER 16

Rehabilitation of Sports Injuries

When one of your athletes has had an injury of any consequence, he or she will require a period of rehabilitation before reentering practice or competition. Failure to properly rehabilitate an injury may place the athlete at high risk for reinjury.

If athletes have been out of sports for a period of weeks, they may not only need to rehabilitate the injured part, but may also need to repeat the preseason conditioning program. Only when athletes are fully rehabilitated should they be permitted to return to competition.

Sports medicine physicians and athletic trainers are well acquainted with the proper techniques of rehabilitation. Physicians who do not specialize in sports medicine, however, may not be familiar with these techniques. Understanding the goals of rehabilitation in their proper sequence will help you (and perhaps the athlete's physician) in the rehabilitation process. The rehabilitation program should be designed by physicians and trainers and executed by trainers or coaches. Although in many cases you may not have the equipment or know-how to supervise the rehabilitation of a serious injury, it is vital that you understand the process involved. For less serious injuries, such as an ankle or wrist sprain, you should be able to supervise the rehabilitation program by following the procedures described next.

Goals of Rehabilitation

The rehabilitation process aims to achieve four goals in the following sequence:

Range of motion

Endurance

Strength

Skill

Only when the athlete has attained a specific proficiency in the first goal is he or she to start working on the next goal, and so on. If the program is rushed or not followed in sequence, the rehabilitation period may be unnecessarily prolonged or the athlete reinjured. The methods of obtaining these goals may vary from program to program depending on the facilities available.

In addition to various exercises, the rehabilitation program may use ultrasound or electrogalvanic stimulation and various sophisticated exercise programs that use high speed, isokinetic, or negative work. These programs are beyond the scope of this text and should be left to the athletic trainer and sports medicine physician.

Cryotherapy, or using an ice pack or ice massage on the injured area before the rehabilitation exercises, is helpful. The ice decreases pain and stiffness, allowing the athlete to work more comfortably during the rehabilitation session. Treat the injury with ice 15-20 minutes before the exercise session. Now let's consider each of the four goals more carefully.

Range of Motion

After the injured limb has lost most of its pain and swelling, it is time to start moving it to regain its original range of motion. A parent, the athlete, or you can carry out the rehabilitation program, depending on the

NOW THAT DIDN'T HURT DID IT?

nature of the injury. The limb should have an ice pack applied to the injured area for 15-20 minutes prior to the rehabilitation session. The limb should then be carefully but firmly moved back and forth to the limits imposed by pain or residual swelling. Do not attempt to force the limb beyond its painful limits of movement. Experiencing slight discomfort with this exercise is fine, but the athlete should not push the exercise to the point of severe pain.

The exercise session should last 5-10 minutes and be repeated 2-3 times a day. Athletes should note a gradual increase in limb mobility. If they do not seem to progress, the trainer or physician must be notified.

Athletes are not ready to proceed to the second phase of the rehabilitation program until 80-90% of their normal, pain-free range of motion has returned. You can determine the normal range of motion for the arms and legs by observing the limits of movement of the uninjured limb. This phase of the program can usually be completed in a few days, but with severe injuries (i.e., post surgery), it may take weeks.

Endurance Exercises

Endurance exercises are the second phase of the rehabilitation program. These exercises use little or no weight, but many repetitions. As with the range of motion exercises, the athlete may experience some discomfort, but should feel no severe pain. If athletes do experience considerable pain, they should return to the range of motion exercises for several more days before beginning the endurance exercises again.

...26,27,28,29,30...

Endurance exercises are to be done daily. The athlete should do at least 30-50 repetitions (one set) of each exercise without resting; then, after a 5-minute rest, he or she should do another set of 30-50 repetitions. Following the same procedures, three sets should be done daily. Endurance exercises can be done using light weight machines, walking, swimming, cycling, or any other means that use a lot of repetitions and little weight (resistance). After a few days, if the athlete finds that the exercises become easier, more weight or resistance should be added. As a general rule, whenever the athlete can do 10-15 extra repetitions, add more weight and have him or her return to 3 sets of the original number of repetitions.

For the arms and legs, it is quite simple to determine whether the athlete is ready to progress to the next phase of rehabilitation: Test the endurance of the uninjured limb. When the injured limb can do 80-90% of the repetitions with the same weight as the uninjured limb, the athlete is ready for the next phase of rehabilitation. The endurance exercises, however, should not be discontinued but done on alternating days with the strength exercises described next.

Strength

This phase of the rehabilitation program uses a larger amount of weight or resistance, so that athletes can only do 10-12 repetitions before their muscles tire. Again, three sets of these exercises should be performed, but only every other day. Again, severe

pain or swelling are signs that the injury is not ready for this phase of rehabilitation. If the athlete has either of these symptoms, he or she should notify the trainer or physician and return to the endurance exercises for several days before attempting this phase again.

If the athlete can perform 3-5 extra repetitions, he or she should increase the resistance or weight slightly and complete three sets of 10-12 repetitions. When the injured limb can comfortably handle 80-90% of the weight that the uninjured limb can lift, then athletes may progress to the next phase. Both the endurance and strength exercises, however, should be continued during the next phase until the injured limb is equal to its uninjured counterpart.

Skill

Before injured athletes can finally return to play, they must reeducate their muscles to perform the specific movements required for the specific sport. For runners, this may only be the ability to run at a single speed around a circular track; for the soccer player, however, this is the ability to run at

varying speeds, accelerate, decelerate, jump, turn, and kick to name a few. These skills need to be practiced carefully under your supervision so that you are satisfied the athlete can perform at 100%.

Guidelines for Rehabilitation of a Minor Ankle Sprain

Because the ankle sprain is so common, we have listed specific guidelines for rehabilitating this injury. The concepts for rehabilitating a sprained ankle apply to other injuries as well.

1. Athletes should not walk on the injured limb if it is so painful as to cause them to limp appreciably. Apply ICE and use crutches.

2. When athletes can walk with a minimal limp, start using 15-20 minutes of ice and have them move the foot up and down and side to side for 5-10 minutes to increase the range of motion. Spelling the alphabet on the floor with the toe is a good exercise.

3. When athletes can start to walk without a limp, they may start some easy jogging in a straight line. They could also cycle to keep in shape.

4. When athletes can jog without pain, they should start running some slow, large figure eight exercises. With each day, they should increase the speed of running and make the figure eight smaller.

5. When athletes can do a small, full-speed figure eight while running, they should begin sharp cutting to left and right as well as quick starts and stops.

6. Athletes can return to play if they can complete the fifth goal as well as hop easily on the injured limb and jog down a set of stairs without a limp.

Athletes should attain each goal before moving to the next, more difficult, goal. If they have any pain or develop additional swelling from performing one of these exercises, they should go back to the previous exercise for a few days before trying that particular goal again. Each injury is different, and you may find that an athlete may progress from the first to the sixth goal in a few days or a few weeks, depending on the severity of the injury. Pain and swelling are good guides to help the athlete advance along this program: They should not occur if the program is conducted at the proper rate and sequence. If athletes get "stuck" at one certain level, they should be reevaluated by the trainer or physician.

Cardiovascular and General Muscular Fitness During Prolonged Injury

If athletes are incapacitated for several weeks, they may want to maintain some of their conditioning despite their temporary handicap. You should encourage this as long as exercising does not cause additional risk of injury or new injury. Although athletes may be unable to walk or bear weight on an injured leg, they may be able to swim, row, cycle, or lift weights. A suitable program can be arrived at by combining the athlete's enthusiasm, your ingenuity, and the physician's consent.

Key Points to Remember

1. For any significant injury, proper rehabilitation is essential before the athlete returns to play.

2. The four goals of rehabilitation are range of motion, endurance, strength, and skill and they should be followed in that sequence.

3. Before rehabilitating athletes for range of motion, apply an ice pack to the injured area for 15-20 minutes. Then, carefully but firmly move the limb back and forth for 5-10 minutes, 2-3 times a day, until athletes have regained 80-90% of their normal, pain-free range of motion.

4. Endurance exercises, such as using light weights, walking, swimming, or cycling, employ little or no weight, but many repetitions.

5. Strength exercises use a large amount of weight or resistance and only 10-12 repetitions. Athletes should perform three sets of 10-12 repetitions every other day.

6. Skills rehabilitation requires that athletes reeducate their muscles to perform specific skills of their sport. Athletes must practice these skills until the coach is satisfied that they can perform at 100%.

7. Athletes' failure to make steady progress on a rehabilitation program is an indication for further evaluation by a physician.

PART 6

Other Useful Information

CHAPTER 17
You and the Law

CHAPTER 18
A Parent Orientation Program

In Part 6, we turn our attention away from sports medicine and science to other important matters pertaining to coaching. We asked Professor Gary Nygaard to write chapter 17, "You and the Law," because you should know what your legal responsibilities are, whether you are a paid or volunteer coach. As you read this chapter, notice that if you practice what we preached in Parts 1 through 5, you will be much less likely to experience any legal problems.

In chapter 18 we present the contents of a Parent Orientation Program to help you establish positive relationships with the parents of your athletes. As veteran youth sports coaches know full well, cooperating with parents is essential for a successful program.

We conclude *Coaching Young Athletes* with three appendices, all listing sources for additional information. In Appendix A we provide you with additional references on the topic of youth sports in general as well as on the five sports medicine and science topics discussed in this book. Appendix B contains a list of publications we recommend to you for the teaching of technique in many sports. And finally, Appendix C is a list of the major youth sports organizations in the United States.

CHAPTER 17

You and the Law

by Gary Nygaard

When you become a coach, you assume some new legal responsibilities, regardless of whether you get paid for coaching or are a volunteer. This chapter will examine your legal responsibilities or duties and discuss how the law will view your actions or inactions.

People are suing people and institutions for nearly everything today. A student sought $853,000 in part for the mental anguish of receiving a "D" in a course rather than the expected "A." A California man sued a would-be companion for standing him up on a date. An Arkansas woman sued because she injured herself when a toilet seat slipped while she was standing rather than sitting on the dirty seat.

In the past, lawsuits were rare in sports; today, they are numerous, and occur for all types of reasons. The makers of sports equipment frequently have been sued, especially manufacturers of football helmets. Coaches have been sued for failing to supervise activities properly, teaching skills improperly, and failing to render first aid properly. And fans have even brought suit against official's calls which caused their teams to lose important games.

Although we don't want to unduly alarm you about your chances of becoming involved in a lawsuit as a result of

Gary Nygaard is a professor of physical education at the University of Montana. He has just completed a book entitled *Law for Physical Educators and Coaches*, which is his field of specialization.

your coaching, we do want you to know why you could potentially be sued. With this knowledge, and by putting into practice the guidelines throughout this book, you will greatly reduce the likelihood of ever making a court appearance.

Negligence

When coaches are sued, the action usually stems from negligence. Negligence is the failure to exercise a reasonable or ordinary amount of care in a situation that causes harm to someone or something. *Negligence occurs when you fail to perform a legally owed duty as would a reasonable and prudent coach, with this failure resulting in actual damage that is a consequence of your breach of duty and that should have been foreseen.*

When a coach is sued for negligence, he or she has four usual defenses:

1. To prove that any of the elements in the definition of negligence given above was not present. All elements of the definition must be present for there to be negligence.

2. To show that the direct cause of an injury is an act of God, due to the forces of nature.

3. To show that the athlete was guilty of contributory negligence, which simply means he or she contributed to cause the harm suffered. In some states, negligence by both the athlete and the coach must be compared, and any damages awarded on a proportionate basis.

4. To prove that an element of risk is always inherent in sport, and if a player knows, understands, and appreciates these risks and proceeds to engage in the activity, he or she assumes those risks. It must be emphasized that a player only assumes those risks that are *inherent* in a sport. In

football, for example, being tackled is an inherent risk, but being tackled on a dangerous surface is not. An inherent risk is one that is derived and inseparable from playing the game.

When coaches are sued, the action usually stems from negligence.

General and Specific Supervision

When coaching, you have both general and specific supervision duties. General supervision is your responsibility to be in the area of play. Three guidelines are suggested for meeting this responsibility:*

1. You should be immediately accessible to the activity and be able to oversee the entire program systematically.

2. You must be alert to conditions which may be dangerous to participants and take action to protect them.

3. You must be able to react immediately and appropriately to emergencies.

Unlike general supervision, specific supervision requires you to be with the individuals participating. Specific supervision refers to the planning, direction, and evaluation of an activity. It means direct supervision at the immediate location of an activity and is more action-oriented. For example, as your players move from light warm-up activities to practice or a game, specific supervision is likely to be required of you. Two guidelines for when specific supervision must be given are:

1. When you are introducing an activity, until players are familiar enough with the activity to appreciate their own ability to do the activity, and are able to understand and adhere to the safety procedures established;

2. When you observe any failure to adhere to rules or any change in the condition of the players.*

The more dangerous the activity, the more specific the supervision required. General supervision may be adequate for a playground, but not for your football team.

An example of inappropriate supervision occurred when two students who were boxing had received no warnings about the risks in boxing. In addition, they had received no training in the skills of boxing. They were simply allowed to engage in a slugging match, during which time the teacher was not in the ring nor directly supervising. Instead, he sat in the bleachers and watched. One of the boxers suffered a cerebral hemorrhage, brought suit, and the teacher was found guilty of negligence.

Coaches' Legal Duties

You have at least nine important duties as a coach from a legal point of view. They are to:

1. Provide a safe environment.

2. Properly plan the activity.

3. Evaluate students for injury or incapacity.

4. Match or equate students.

5. Provide adequate and proper equipment.

6. Warn of inherent risks in the sport.

7. Supervise the activity closely.

8. Know emergency procedures and first aid.

9. Keep adequate records.

These duties are to be met in both general and specific supervisory situations, but are more critical in those circumstances requiring specific supervision. We will discuss each of these duties briefly, presenting examples of negligence in meeting them. Some of the lawsuits described involve older participants, but the principles apply to coaches of young athletes for whom the standard of care is sometimes even higher.

Provide a Safe Environment

Coaches frequently are sued on charges that a facility, piece of apparatus, or equipment was unsafe. For example, in a football lawsuit, a field was lined with unslaked lime. During the course of play, one player's face was forced into the lime, resulting in the loss of sight in one eye and seriously impaired vision in the other.

As a coach you have the duty to *regularly* and *thoroughly* inspect the facility area, apparatus, and equipment to be used. How regularly and how thoroughly depends on the activity and experience of the players. The greater the risk in an activity, the more regular and thorough should be your inspections. At the very least, inspection should be made at the beginning, middle, and end of a season. Inspections of dangerous equipment such as trampolines or protective devices such as football helmets should be continuous, and prudent coaches will develop with their players a "shared

---

*Van Der Smissen, B. Legal aspects of adult fitness programs. *Selected problems in sport safety*. Washington, DC: AAHPER, 1975.

responsibility" for inspecting these items.

To fulfill your duty for providing a safe environment, you have the responsibility to "notice" hazards. Legally, there are two kinds of notice: actual and constructive. If you see and remedy a hazard you have fulfilled your duty of *actual notice*. The more troublesome concept is *constructive notice*. Under this concept, you may be liable for a condition you should have noticed, but did not.

This was the situation in a recent softball case in which a small block of concrete between second and third base was somehow not noticed, and a player fell on it and was injured. The court held that a prudent coach would have noticed the block. In providing a safe environment, not only are you responsible for what is apparent, but also for what the mythical "reasonable and prudent coach" would have noticed.

The objective of providing a safe environment involves:

1. Recognizing and understanding the hazards of all activities and facilities;

2. Removing all unnecessary hazards of facilities, equipment, and programming;

3. Compensating through education and protective equipment for those hazards that cannot be removed;

4. Creating no new hazards.

To avoid lawsuits and minimize the risk of injury, practice the concept of "preventive maintenance," and maintain facilities, apparatus, and equipment.

Properly Plan the Activity

Good coaches plan judiciously, as we emphasized in chapters 7 through 9. Failure to plan carefully may not only impair players' learning but may also result in injury, and thus, a potential lawsuit. When coaching your athletes, one of the most important aspects of planning is the progression of teaching new skills, particularly potentially dangerous skills. Coaches may be subject to lawsuit if they teach a skill which requires, for example, more strength than athletes possess or which grossly exceeds their current skill level. It is the coaches' duty to plan activities which the athletes are physically ready to learn.

One type of planning error resulted in the death of a young boy in a golf class. The original plan for the class had students hitting whiffle balls from mats arranged at one end of the gymnasium. During the class, however, the mats were not arranged in this way. While the teacher was concentrating on one group of students, another student at another mat was instructing a young boy. Lacking previous golf instruction, the boy got too close to the mat and was killed when struck in the head by a golf club. Testimony by an expert witness indicated the original plan and method of instruction should have been followed.

" WE GOTTA GET ORGANIZED HERE!..."

Other cases substantiate this one, indicating that an adequate plan for instruction or coaching be established and followed. An adequate plan is one capable of withstanding professional examination. In this regard, it is the duty of the coach to make sure the plan is up-to-date with current technique. For example, spear tackling in football was recommended by coaches and in textbooks during the 1960s, but it is now widely known for being a dangerous practice. If a coach taught spear tackling today, he or she could risk a lawsuit.

Evaluate Your Athletes for Injury or Incapacity

As a coach, you must consider any injuries or incapacities of your players in directing their participation. Coaches frequently have been sued for coercing or persuading a player to return to play too soon after an injury. An injured athlete should not be expected to do an activity which is potentially harmful. Further, an athlete who has valid apprehensions about an activity should not be forced to do that activity.

A well-known lawsuit in sport and physical education law illustrates this point. In this case, the young girl was trying to do a tumbling stunt known as the "roll over two" and fractured her skull. The girl stated she was taking the class under protest; that she was not directly instructed by the teacher but by advanced students; that in doing this exercise previously she had fallen many times; that she had a bad knee which went out at times; and that 2 weeks before the accident she had fallen in the locker room, injured her knee, and told the teacher that her knee was bad. The court ruled in the girl's favor, holding that her mental and physical condition was not adequate for such activity.

The lesson from this case is simple: To avoid lawsuits do not force or coerce your players to do any activities which they do not want to do, especially if you suspect any type of injury or incapacity.

Match or Equate Athletes

A number of lawsuits allege that athletes have been mismatched when participating in sport. These suits have not been limited to contact sports, but also have occurred in activities like soccer. As discussed in chapter 14, you should not arbitrarily match players for competition. Instead, you should match youngsters on their skill and experience, as well as their age, height, weight, and maturity. Because skill varies from activity to activity, you should avoid regarding a player who is good in one activity as good in all activities.

A number of lawsuits allege that athletes have been mismatched when participating in sport.

A mismatch was held to be part of the cause of negligence in an indoor soccer case. The coach had placed two groups of boys on each side of the gymnasium. One boy in each group was given the same number as a boy in the other group. The coach made no attempt to match the boys on any physical basis. When their number was called, the two boys ran toward a ball equidistant between them and tried to kick it toward the opponent's goal. In doing so, a boy considerably smaller than his matched opponent was injured. The court ruled this method of matching was inadequate and held the coach liable.

In Oregon, a seriously injured football player brought suit for a variety of reasons, one being that the team they were playing was vastly superior and should not have been scheduled. In commenting on this

allegation, the court made this comment:

> It is possible that two football teams may be so disparate in size and ability that those responsible for supervising the athletic program would violate their duty in permitting the teams to play.

Provide Adequate and Proper Equipment

Although this duty sounds obvious, it is occasionally ignored because of expense, inconvenience, or carelessness. You should provide your players with the best equipment your budget allows. The equipment should meet any existing codes or standards, and it must be maintained and repaired so that it is safe for the activity at all times.

In one youth football program, football helmets were distributed on a first-come, first-serve basis. As a result, some of the participants had helmets too small or too large. Those with helmets too small sometimes removed the suspension to make them fit, in essence wearing only the shell. Those with helmets too large sometimes stuffed them with newspaper. In these instances, the helmets were inadequate protective devices for the sport of football.

The law says you must be diligent in the manner in which you select, distribute, use, and repair equipment. If equipment is used, it must be used properly. Some equipment has guidelines for its use. For example, the

National Operating Committee for Standards in Athletic Equipment (NOCSAE) has published recommendations for football helmets. You and your players should follow these recommendations, thus sharing the responsibility for safety. If equipment is not used, it should be kept inaccessible so as not to create a hazard or an attractive nuisance.

Warn of Inherent Risks of a Sport

Athletes only assume those risks which are an inherent part of a sport, and only when they know, understand, and appreci-

"DID I FORGET TO WARN YOU ABOUT THE HOLE IN THE PRACTICE FIELD?"

ate those risks. Prudent coaches explain the particular risks of an activity so that their players will be aware of those risks before accepting them. It is not exactly clear what degree of understanding and appreciation athletes must have, but a single verbal warning may be inadequate.

An interesting example of the importance of warnings is a case in which an experienced high school baseball player was severely injured while attempting to score on a squeeze play. The batter took a full swing and missed the ball entirely. The catcher caught the pitch and moved out to block home plate. The baserunner dove into the catcher head first and injured himself.

In the lawsuit, the injured athlete admitted that the coach had taught the correct technique (feet-first slide), but did not warn against the consequences of using other, untaught, techniques. Further, in a similar play 2 weeks before the injury, the injured player had used his shoulder to bowl over a catcher and score the run—after which the coach allegedly praised him for his play. In spite of the injured player's experience, because he had only been taught the feet-first slide and not warned about the head-first slide, the jury awarded over $1,000,000 to the player and his parents.

Although you may disagree with such a ruling, this case illustrates how the courts require coaches to be more thorough and more explicit when warning players about the risks in a sport.

Supervise the Activity Closely

You may be found negligent if one of your athletes is injured and the cause of the injury can be related to your lack of supervision. Although you are not expected to personally observe everything and guarantee the safety of the players, the courts consider the type of supervision, the location of the coaches, and the competency of the

coaches in determining negligence.

The best advice we can give you is to follow the guidelines for supervision presented in this and other chapters of the book. In addition, recognize that each sport has its own specific supervisory requirements. We cannot list all of them here because they depend on the sport you are coaching. It should be clear, however, that you cannot take your supervisory skills lightly—the courts certainly will not.

Know Emergency Procedures

All coaches should have complete command of the information in chapter 15 on first aid and should keep up-to-date with these procedures. In addition, every coach or league should have a procedure established for seeking necessary medical care for injured athletes. At the very least, you should be able to protect injured players from further harm, maintain or attempt to restore life, comfort and reassure them, and activate an emergency medical system.

A number of lawsuits illustrate the failure to fulfill this duty. In one case, a quarterback was injured during a preseason interschool scrimmage. The player was lying on his back and unable to get to his feet. The coach suspected a neck injury and had the player take hold of his hands to determine his ability to grip. Because the player was able to do so, he was then improperly carried off the field under the coach's direction. No stretcher or backboard was used, but eight boys, four on each side, carried him. After the player was moved off the field, the grip test was again administered, and the player was unable to move his hands, fingers, and feet. A physician testified that it was his opinion that the injured player must have sustained additional damage to the spinal cord when moved from the field. The jury returned a verdict in favor of the injured player in the sum of $325,000.

A report should be made of any serious injury among your players.

In another football case, a player collapsed during football practice, was put on the bus and brought back to the school. He was given a shower and then placed on the floor with a blanket over him. During this time the boy's condition worsened, so the coaches consulted a first aid manual and discussed what to do. A parent of another player arrived and observed that the boy was severely ill. This was an hour and a half after the boy had collapsed. The parent stated to the coach that the injured player was critical and apparently in shock and that a physician should be called. By the time a physician arrived, 2 hours after the collapse, the player was unconscious, cyanotic, and without a pulse. The doctor diagnosed the condition as profound heat exhaustion with shock to an advanced degree.

Early the next morning, the player died.

The court found that the coaches were negligent because they actively denied the player access to treatment for some 2 hours after the symptoms appeared. The court believed that, more than likely, the player would have survived with reasonably prompt medical attention. We reiterate:

KNOW FIRST AID!

Keep Adequate Records

Many coaches despise record keeping, but it is useful for planning, and essential for obtaining pertinent data about injuries. In light of recent court cases, you are well advised to keep records of your instructional plans (chapters 8 and 9) and injury and accident reports. Keep these records in a safe place.

A report should be made of any serious injury among your players. On page 175 is a standard accident form from the National Safety Council which we recommend you use. This form should be completed as soon after the injury as possible. Your report should be a descriptive and objective observation of the injury and the events surrounding; it should not be a diagnosis. Retain your records for several years, because a minor can bring suit up until 2 to 3 years after reaching the age of majority.

Other Concerns

Transportation

Your major concern here is, of course, safely transporting players to and from games and practices. To do this, you have several options—including the use of public transportation, school transportation, or private transportation. Your legal situation differs for each type of transportation.

STANDARD STUDENT ACCIDENT REPORT FORM
Part A. Information on All Accidents

1. Name: _____ Home Address: _____
2. School _____ Sex M☐ F☐ Age _____ Grade or classification _____
3. Time accident occurred Hour _____ A.M., _____ P.M. Date: _____
4. Place of accident: School Building☐ School Grounds☐ To or from School☐ Home☐ Elsewhere☐

PART OF BODY INJURED

Abrasion	___	Fracture	___
Amputation	___	Laceration	___
Asphyxiation	___	Poisoning	___
Bite	___	Puncture	___
Bruise	___	Scalds	___
Burn	___	Scratches	___
Concussion	___	Shock (el.)	___
Cut	___	Sprain	___
Dislocation	___		
Other (specify) _____			

DESCRIPTION OF THE ACCIDENT

How did accident happen? What was student doing? Where was student? List specifically unsafe acts and unsafe conditions existing. Specify any tool, machine or equipment involved.

_____
_____
_____
_____
_____

NATURE OF INJURY

Abdomen	___	Foot	___
Ankle	___	Hand	___
Arm	___	Head	___
Back	___	Knee	___
Chest	___	Leg	___
Ear	___	Mouth	___
Elbow	___	Nose	___
Eye	___	Scalp	___
Face	___	Tooth	___
Finger	___	Wrist	___
Other (specify) _____			

_____
_____
_____
_____
_____
_____
_____

6. Degree of Injury: Death☐ Permanent Impairment☐ Temporary Disability☐ Nondisabling☐
7. Total number of days lost from school _____ (To be filled in when student returns to school)

Part B. Additional Information on School Jurisdiction Accidents

8. Teacher in charge when accident occurred (Enter name) _____
   Present at scene of accident: No _____ Yes _____

IMMEDIATE ACTION TAKEN

First-aid treatment	_____	By (Name): _____
Sent to school nurse	_____	By (Name): _____
Sent home	_____	By (Name): _____
Sent to physician	_____	By (Name): _____
		Physician's Name: _____
Sent to hospital	_____	By (Name): _____
		Name of hospital: _____

10. Was a parent or other individual notified? No ___ Yes ___ When _____ How _____
    Name of individual notified: _____
    By whom? (Enter name): _____
11. Witnesses: 1. Name: _____ Address: _____
    2. Name: _____ Address: _____

LOCATION

	Specify Activity		Specify Activity
Athletic field	_____	Locker	_____
Auditorium	_____	Pool	_____
Cafeteria	_____	Sch. grounds	_____
Classroom	_____	___ shop	_____
Corridor	_____	Showers	_____
Dressing room	_____	Stairs	_____
Gymnasium	_____	Toilets and	
Home Econ.	_____	washrooms	_____
Laboratories	_____	Other (specify)	_____

Remarks

What recommendations do you have for preventing other accidents of this type?

_____
_____
_____
_____
_____

Signed: Principal: _____ Teacher: _____

Perhaps the best way to travel, in terms of reducing your liability, is via public transportation. Use it if it is available and affordable.

School coaches more typically transport athletes in school cars or school buses. The responsibility for maintaining these vehicles rests with the schools, as does the responsibility for having qualified drivers for the vehicles. If you ever drive a school vehicle, it may be necessary for you to have a chauffeur's license.

When you use your own car to transport athletes, it must be properly inspected and in satisfactory condition. And, of course, you should have adequate and proper insurance. If you are being reimbursed for the use of your car, you may be a carrier of sorts, with need for additional insurance. Check with your auto insurance agent to determine your protection when transporting athletes in your automobile.

Waivers and Releases

It is quite common for players who are about to take part in an activity to sign a statement indicating that the sponsoring agency and its agents, including the coaches, will be free from liability in case of an injury. In some cases, especially with minors, the parents are also asked to sign, thereby agreeing to the statement. Such statements, although varying in detail, are similar to the following:

> I hereby, for myself, my heirs, executors and administrators, waive and release any and all right and claims for damage I may have against the (agency) and all tournament sponsors, and their respective representives for any and all injuries which may be suffered by me in connection with any participation in this tournament.
>
> Signature _____
>
> Parent (if minor) _____

These statements are usually called waivers, releases, disclaimers, or parental permission slips.

Such waivers seem to offer little legal protection from lawsuit for several reasons. First, a waiver is regarded as a form of contract, and a minor cannot contract legally. A signed waiver by a minor is worthless, for he or she may still bring lawsuit 2 to 3 years after reaching legal age and becoming capable of such legal decisions. Further, even if a minor signs a waiver or release, his or her parents can still bring suit. If both the minor and the parents sign a waiver, the parents may relinquish their rights to recover damages, but they still may not waive negligence which injures the minor. A child may still be able to sue after he or she reaches full age. A waiver will not release a coach from negligence, as coaches generally have the responsibility not to let players involve themselves in considerable risk.

Liability waivers seem to offer little legal protection from lawsuit.

A second objection to such waivers is that such an agreement may tend to produce a lack of care. Those responsible for a program may not be as diligent as possible in providing safe conditions if they know they are not liable for any injuries.

A final objection to the waiver is simply based on the legal opinion that no individual may contract against his or her own negligence. A waiver, in essence, would free one from liability for future actions, and because no one can predict future action with great accuracy, any such contract is questionable and unwise.

Our advice is to forget the use of waivers.

Safety Guidelines

You now should be aware of your legal

duties as a coach. In order to reduce both injury to your athletes as well as the likelihood of a lawsuit against you, follow these guidelines:

1. Establish procedures for accidents and emergencies, including appropriate report forms. Safety rules and regulations should be included in these procedures and enforced in the programs.

2. Establish an adequate plan of supervision and make certain that those who assist you are competent to do so.

3. Regularly and thoroughly inspect facilities, apparatus, and equipment, and establish a program of preventive maintenance.

4. Plan instruction and competition by taking into account individual differences in skill and experience. Be careful to teach skills in their proper progression.

5. In case of injury, do not force first aid upon an athlete if they resist. Render only emergency first aid treatment. Call a physician immediately, and notify the player's parents. Take extreme care if the potential

for injury to the spinal cord exists. If you are uncertain about a neck or back injury, leave the injured athlete in place until qualified personnel come to move the youngster.

6. Complete an injury report as soon as possible. An example of an accident report form is on page 175.

7. Ensure that your players are safely transported to and from games and practices. The best way to travel in terms of reducing your liability is by public transportation; the most common, however, is by school cars or buses. Make sure that the drivers of the school vehicles are qualified. If you must use your own car, be sure that it is in good condition, and that both you and your car are properly insured.

8. Have both your players and the parents of your players sign a waiver releasing you from liability in case of injury. These waivers, however, offer little protection in legal cases and may even cause coaches to be less than diligent in providing safe conditions for their athletes. Thus, we do not encourage the use of waivers.

CHAPTER 18

A Parent Orientation Program

Developing a good working relationship with the parents of your athletes is almost as important as the relationship you develop with the athletes themselves. With a little effort you can have parents working with you and appreciating your efforts. The key is to tell them about your program and to listen to their concerns. We have found that many of the problems between parents and coaches can be avoided if coaches hold a Parent Orientation Program prior to the season. This program can serve a number of useful purposes, including:

- Enabling parents to understand the objectives of the program.

- Allowing parents to become acquainted with you, the person responsible for their son or daughter.

- Informing parents about the nature of the sport.

- Informing parents about what is expected of their youngster and what is expected of them.

- Enabling you to understand parents' concerns.

- Establishing clear lines of communication between you and the parents.

- Obtaining support from parents in helping to conduct the season's activities.

Neglecting to conduct a Parent Orientation Program is easy; it takes even more of your time, and you already are overextended. You may feel uncomfortable in front of an adult group. And anyway, you volunteered to coach young athletes, not adults. But in spite of the hassle or your reluctance, conducting a Parent Orientation Program is important and valuable. Veteran coaches know the importance of open, honest communication between parents and coach in having a successful and enjoyable program. To help you conduct a Parent Orientation Program, we have prepared this chapter.

Planning the Program

When should the meeting be held? Schedule the meeting as early in the season as possible. The meeting may be held before the first practice if most members of the team have been identified, or it may be held 1 or 2 weeks after initial practices have begun. Find a time when most parents can attend and invite all parents individually by phone or personal letter.

A Parent Orientation Meeting is very important to the success of your season.

How long should the meeting be? Two hours or less will be needed to accomplish the objectives previously stated.

Should the athletes attend the meeting? Coaches have mixed opinions about this. Some think it may inhibit communication between parent and coach, whereas others believe that it may help improve communication between parent, coach, and athlete. This is a decision you will need to make based on your coaching philosophy.

Where should the meeting be held? Select a location easily accessible to the parents. Be sure the room is suitable for your purposes, that it is well lighted, and has enough space and comfortable seating.

How should the meeting be conducted? First, be well prepared and organized. Get started on time and keep the program moving along. Based on interviews with parents and coaches, we have developed a format you may wish to use in conducting a Parent Orientation Program. Coaches may find that not all aspects of the program are needed in their particular situation or that other topics need to be included. This outline is intended only as a guide and should be adjusted to meet the needs of each coach's situation.

Parent Orientation Program Agenda

Coach Introduction (5 minutes)

Introduce yourself and any assistant coaches so that parents know who you are and what qualifies you to receive their trust in coaching their son or daughter. You might give a little background about yourself—why you're coaching, your experience in the sport, and what you do for a living.

Coaching Philosophy (10 minutes)

Next, a brief discussion by you about your philosophy of coaching will be helpful. You might want to reread Part 1 to prepare. Be sure to at least discuss the following points:

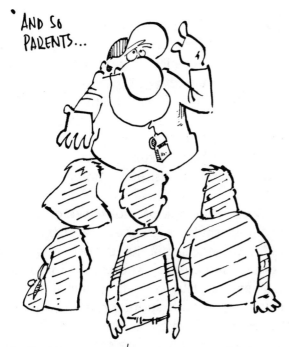

"AND SO PARENTS...

AS I ONCE TOLD VINCE LOMBARDI, I SAID, "VINCE!".. "WINNING ISN'T EVERYTHING."

1. The value of this sport for youngsters; that is, what you hope will be the benefits of this sport for the youngsters.

2. The methods you use to teach skills. You might describe what you do in a typical practice.

3. The emphasis you give winning, having fun, and the development of youngsters physically and psychologically.

4. What you expect of each athlete. You may wish to do this by discussing some of your team rules and guidelines if you have them.

Demonstration or Film (30 minutes)

Parents may know little about the sport you're coaching. To assist them in understanding and appreciating the sport, a demonstration of the conduct, scoring, and rules may be helpful—and appreciated. You may want to use the entire team or select a few youngsters to assist you in the demonstration. Keep the demonstration simple, showing how the sport is played and scored.

The beginning of the demonstration is an opportune time to discuss the equipment needed for the sport. Emphasis should be given to safety when discussing equipment and the rules. Don't forget to mention the importance of the referee in ensuring the safety of their son or daughter. If you cannot arrange a demonstration, perhaps you can locate a good film. Many national youth sports agencies have films that you may be able to borrow.

The Specifics of Your Program (15 minutes)

Now you are ready to describe the specific program you will be conducting. Here are some things which parents will want to know. You may think of some others.

- How much time will their son or daughter be with you?

- How often do the youngsters practice?

- How long is the season?

- How many contests will there be?

- How do you decide who plays and who doesn't?

- How frequently does the team travel and who pays for the expense?

- What equipment do they need to purchase for their youngster?

- Where do they buy equipment and how much does it cost?

Other specific details of your program can be also discussed at this time. You may wish to talk about obtaining a medical, insurance, and fund-raising projects, for example.

Question-Answer Session (30-45 minutes)

You've been doing most of the talking up to this point. Now it is time to let the parents ask some questions. A number of questions that parents may ask (or at least should ask) are subsequently listed. If parents don't raise these questions, you should. We have provided a few comments for each question to help you prepare your answers. Keep in mind, however, that not all questions pertain to every sport.

Should my child have a medical examination before competing? You should have a policy on this. If not, you should develop one. The American Medical Association recommends that a child should have a medical examination at least once a year (see chapter 14).

Is my child ready to compete in this sport? Determining whether a youngster is ready *physically* to begin participating in this sport is ultimately the parents' decision, but they can get help from their physician and from you as an experienced coach. Once the youngster comes out for your team, it is your responsibility to make sure he or she is physically prepared through proper conditioning and skill instruction.

Determining whether a youngster is ready *psychologically* to compete is best determined by the child. If children express an interest, show enthusiasm for participating, they are ready. Children who are pushed into the sport by peers or adults will also need to be pushed into practice. They are not ready!

Should boys compete with girls? Before puberty, there are no physical reasons why boys and girls should not compete together. Girls, in fact, tend to be a little more mature physically than boys and they often do quite well against boys of the same age. Around the age of 10-12 years, though, pubescence occurs and girls begin developing adult female characteristics. It is not recommended that postpubescent girls compete with postpubescent boys in sports involving speed, power, or strength. The physical changes experienced by boys and girls as they go through puberty result in boys usually having a decided physical advantage.

What is the risk of injury? We don't have accurate statistics on the rate of injuries in different sports. Injuries do occur, more in contact and collision sports than in noncontact sports. But overall, children in well-supervised youth sports programs in which coaches take the precautions recommended throughout this book are safer than children riding their bicycles or skateboards.

Who decides when my child is ready to return to competition after being injured? Obviously, the parent is ultimately responsible. When a serious injury has occurred, a physician should be consulted before the youngster returns to participation. You, as the coach, also have the prerogative to withhold athletes from competition if you believe they are not ready.

What are reasonable expectations for us to have of our child at this age? Coaches play a most important part in helping parents to develop reasonable expectations for their children. All too often problems occur when parents hold one expectation and coaches another, and sometimes the athletes still another. Parents sometimes think their children are more capable than they are, and when the youngsters don't achieve what the parents want them to achieve, they look for faults in the youngsters or the coach. Probably the one topic you'll discuss most with parents during the season is the expectations you and the parents should have for the youngster.

Should we attend practice sessions? Contests? We suggest that you decide whether you want parents at practice sessions. Certainly under normal circumstances, it is desirable to have parents attend the contests. Under certain circumstances, such as when a child becomes particularly anxious when parents are present, it may be wise to recommend that parents do not attend.

Should we talk with our son or daughter during the contest? This question opens the door to the whole issue of parental behavior during competitive meets. We suggest that you develop some guidelines for parental behavior. Perhaps you will want to suggest that they not attempt to coach their child from the sideline, that they not yell negative remarks to any athlete, and that they praise the effort not the outcome.

Does my child need any special precontest meal? Athletes should eat a well-balanced diet at least 3 hours before competition, avoiding high fat foods (see chapter 13).

Can we do anything at home to facilitate our child's physical development or the learning of the sport skills? Again, you will need to decide whether or not you wish to have parents attempting to supplement what you are doing. Many coaches are opposed to parents doing this unless they are uniquely qualified because they may teach skills incorrectly, making the task that much more difficult for you.

What do we do when our child loses? Wins? Parents play an important role in helping children interpret their experiences. Parents can help a child understand the significance of winning and losing, of experiencing frustration in learning, and the need for developing self-confidence, a desire to achieve, and self-appreciation. Sport can be an important activity that opens up lines of communication between parent and child if parents take the opportunity to be interested in their child's participation. Parents need to recognize that sports induce intense emotions; children sometimes cry when they lose. You should help parents understand the emotions associated with sport.

What expectations do you have of us? You should convey to the parents what assistance you will need from them during the season. You will need their support and reinforcement of the program objectives. If you have not already done so, you should specify what you consider to be appropriate behavior for parents at contests. You may also mention that parents play a vital role in encouraging their child during the season, that they can help their child in understanding the significance of winning and losing, and the emotions associated with competitive sports.

What expectations can we have of you? In part you will have answered this throughout the evening, but you may wish to summarize what the parents can expect from you. Remember, throughout the season parents will observe you directly or indirectly through their child and will compare what you *say* you do with what you actually *do*. Be prepared to be consistent.

How do we contact you if we have a concern? Indicate how you wish parents to communicate with you. You may want to plan additional meetings. Some coaches have found it highly beneficial to have a midseason meeting with parents to discuss their child's progress and then to have a postseason banquet to recognize all youngsters' accomplishments.

A Final Suggestion

At the end of the season, invite each parent to evaluate you and the program.

Ask them to point out things that went well and those that could be improved. If you want to, you can use the following evalua- tion form. Give a copy to each parent and ask them to return it to you. It may help you become a better coach!

Postseason Parent Evaluation Form

A. Evaluate the degree to which you believe your son or daughter achieved the following (Circle one):

	Very much		Somewhat		Not at all
My child had fun.	1	2	3	4	5
My child learned the fundamentals of the sport.	1	2	3	4	5

B. Evaluate the degree to which you believe your child changed on the following characteristics (Circle one):

	Improved/ Increased	No change	Declined/ Decreased	Don't Know
Physical fitness	I	NC	D	DK
Learning to cooperate	I	NC	D	DK
Self-confidence	I	NC	D	DK
Desire to continue to play this sport	I	NC	D	DK
Development of self-reliance	I	NC	D	DK
Learning specific skills of this sport	I	NC	D	DK
Leadership skills	I	NC	D	DK
Sportsman-like behavior	I	NC	D	DK
Development of initiative	I	NC	D	DK
Learning to compete	I	NC	D	DK

C. How did the coach do on the following items? (Circle one):

	Excellent	Good	So-So	Weak	Poor	Don't Know
Treated your child fairly	E	G	SS	W	P	DK
Kept winning in perspective	E	G	SS	W	P	DK
Took safety precautions	E	G	SS	W	P	DK
Organized practice and contests	E	G	SS	W	P	DK
Communicated with you	E	G	SS	W	P	DK
Was effective in teaching skills	E	G	SS	W	P	DK
Encouraged your child	E	G	SS	W	P	DK
Recognized your child as a unique individual	E	G	SS	W	P	DK
Held your child's respect	E	G	SS	W	P	DK

D. Please give any additional comments in the space below and on the back. Perhaps you have some constructive criticism or praise you want to offer.

Appendices

Appendix A
Sports Medicine and Science References

Appendix B
Specific Sports Technique References

Appendix C
Major Youth Sports Organizations

APPENDIX A

Sports Medicine and Science References

General

Broadus, C., & Broadus, L. *Laughing and crying with little league.* New York: Harper & Row, 1972.

Magill, R.A., Ash, M.J., & Smoll, F.L. (Eds.). *Children in sport: A contemporary anthology.* Champaign, IL: Human Kinetics, 1978.

Martens, R. (Ed.). *Joy and sadness in children's sports.* Champaign, IL: Human Kinetics, 1978.

Orlick, T., & Botterill, C. *Every kid can win.* Chicago: Nelson-Hall, 1975.

Thomas, J.R. *Youth sports guide: For coaches and parents.* Washington, DC: AAHPER, 1977.

Tutko, T., & Bruns, W. *Winning is everything and other American myths.* New York: Macmillan, 1976.

Sport Philosophy

Ferrell, J., Glashagel, J., & Johnson, M. *A family approach to youth sports.* LaGrange, IL: Youth Sports Press, 1978.

Martens, R., & Seefeldt, V. *Guidelines for children's sports.* Washington, DC: AAHPERD, 1979.

Paulson, W. *Coaching cooperative youth sports: A values education approach.* LaGrange, IL: Youth Sports Press, 1980.

Sessoms, B. *The volunteer coach.* Nashville, TN: Convention Press, 1978.

Warner, G. *Competition.* Elgin, IL: David C. Cook, 1979.

Sport Psychology

Gallwey, W.T. *Inner tennis: Playing the game.* New York: Random House, 1976.

Nideffer, R.M. *The inner athlete: Mind plus muscle for winning.* New York: Crowell, 1976.

Orlick, T. *In pursuit of excellence.* Champaign, IL: Human Kinetics, 1980.

Smoll, F.L., & Smith, R.E. *Improving relationship skills in youth sport coaches.* East Lansing, MI: Institute for the Study of Youth Sports, State of Michigan, 1979.

Tutko, T., & Tosi, U. *Sports psyching: Playing your best game all of the time.*

Los Angeles: J.P. Tarcher, 1976.

Sport Pedagogy

Dougherty, N.J., & Bonanno, D. *Contemporary approaches to the teaching of physical education.* Minneapolis: Burgess, 1979.

Lawther, J.D. *The learning and performance of physical skills* (2nd ed.). Englewood Cliffs, NJ: Prentice-Hall, 1977.

Magill, R.A. *Motor learning: Concepts and applications.* Dubuque, IA: Brown, 1980

Singer, R.N. *Motor learning and human performance: An application to motor and movement behaviors.* New York: Macmillan, 1980.

Singer, R.N., & Dick, W. *Teaching physical education: A systems approach.* Boston: Houghton Mifflin, 1980.

Sport Physiology

Briggs, G.M., & Calloway, D.H. *Bogert's nutrition and physical fitness* (10th ed.).

Philadelphia: Saunders, 1979.

Fox, E.L. *Sports physiology.* Philadelphia: Saunders, 1979.

Sharkey, B.J. *Physiology of fitness.* Champaign, IL: Human Kinetics, 1979.

Smith, N.J. *Food for sport.* Palo Alto, CA: Bull, 1976.

Wilmore, J.H. *Athletic training and physical fitness: Physiological principles and practices of the conditioning process.* Boston: Allyn & Bacon, 1976.

Sports Medicine

Dominguez, R.H. *The complete book of sports medicine.* New York: Scribner, 1979.

Donahue, P. *Sports doc: Medical advice, diet, fitness tips and other essential hints for young athletes.* New York: Knopf, 1979.

Fahey, T.D. *What to do about athletic injuries.* New York: Butterick, 1979.

Klafs, C.E., & Arnheim, D.D. *Modern principles of athletic training* (5th ed.). St. Louis: Mosby, 1981.

Rawlinson, K. *Modern athletic training.* North Palm Beach, FL: Athletic Institute, 1980.

APPENDIX B

Specific Sports Technique References

Baseball

Depel, J. *The baseball handbook for coaches and players.* New York: Scribner, 1976.

Litwhiler, D. *Treasury of baseball drills.* West Nyak, NY: Parker, 1979.

Nitardy, W.J. *Baseball coaching techniques* (2nd rev. ed.). San Diego: Barnes, 1980.

Basketball

Basketball Clinic (Eds.). *The Basketball Clinic's treasury of drills.* West Nyak, NY: Parker, 1977.

Ebert, F., & Cheatum, B.A. *Basketball.* Philadelphia: Saunders, 1977.

Ferrell, J. (Ed.). *Youth Basketball Association leader's manual.* Colorado Springs, CO: National Board of YMCAs, 1979.

Jeremiah, M. *Coaching basketball: Ten winning concepts.* New York: Wiley, 1979.

Bowling

Barsanti, R.A. *Bowling.* Boston: Allyn & Bacon, 1974.

Dolan, E.F. *The complete beginner's guide to bowling.* Garden City, NY: Doubleday, 1974.

James, S. *Bowlers' guide.* Greendale, WI: American Bowling Congress and Women's International Bowling Congress, 1976.

Johnson, D., & Patterson, J. *Inside bowling.* Chicago: Contemporary Books, 1973.

Diving

Armbruster, D.A., Allen, R.H. & Billingsley, H.S. *Swimming and diving* (6th ed.). St. Louis: Mosby, 1973.

Lee, S. *Diving.* New York: Atheneum, 1979.

Smith, D., with Bender, J.H. *Inside diving.* Chicago: Contemporary Books, 1973.

Field Hockey

Flint, R.H. *Field hockey.* Woodbury, NY: Barron, 1978.

Gros, V. *Inside field hockey for women.* Chicago: Contemporary Books, 1979.

Spencer, H.A. *Beginning field hockey.* Belmont, CA: Wadsworth, 1970.

Football

Allen, G. *Handbook of winning football.* Boston: Allyn & Bacon, 1975.

Ferrell, J., & Ferrell, M.A. *Coaching flag football.* Colorado Springs, CO: National Board of YMCAs, 1980.

Friend, J. *Coaching Youth League Football.* North Palm Beach, FL: Athletic Institute, 1980.

Fuoss, D.E. *Championship football drills: For teaching offensive and defensive fundamentals and techniques.* Englewood Cliffs, NJ: Prentice-Hall, 1964.

Golf

Cheatum, B.A. *Golf* (2nd ed.). Philadelphia: Saunders, 1975.

Jacobs, J., & Bowden, K. *Practical golf.* New York: Times, 1976.

Nance, V.L., & Davis, E.C. *Golf* (4th ed.). Dubuque, IA: Brown, 1980.

Gymnastics

Wettstone, E. (Ed.) *Gymnastics safety manual* (2nd ed.). University Park, PA: Pennsylvania State University Press, 1979.

Gymnastics for Boys and Men

Alt, D., with Glossbrenner, A. *Introduction to men's gymnastics.* New York: Hawthorne, 1979.

Arnold, E., & Stocks, B. *Men's gymnastics.* East Ardsley, Wakefield, West Yorkshire, England: E.P. Publishing, 1979.

Kaneko, A. *Olympic gymnastics.* New York: Sterling, 1976.

Gymnastics for Girls and Women

Cooper, P. *Feminine gymnastics* (3rd ed.). Minneapolis: Burgess, 1980.

Murray, M. *Women's gymnastics: Coach, participant, spectator.* Boston: Allyn & Bacon, 1979.

Tonry, D., with Tonry, B. *Sports Illustrated women's gymnastics 1: The floor exercise event.* New York: Lippincott & Crowell, 1980.

Tonry, D., with Tonry, B. *Sports Illustrated women's gymnastics 2: The vaulting, balance beam, and uneven parallel bars events.* New York: Lippincott & Crowell, 1980.

Hockey

Fullerton, J.H. *Ice hockey: Playing and coaching.* New York: Hastings House, 1978.

Kelly, J., & Schmidt, M. *Hockey: Bantam to pro.* Boston: Allyn & Bacon, 1974.

Meagher, J.W. *Coaching hockey: Fundamentals, team play, and techniques.* Englewood Cliffs, NJ: Prentice-Hall, 1972.

Watt, T. *How to play hockey.* New York: Doubleday, 1971.

Ice Skating

DeLeeuw, D., with Lehrman, S. *Figure skating.* New York: Atheneum, 1978.

Fassi, C., with Smith, G. *Skating with Carlo Fassi.* New York: Scribner, 1980.

Racquetball

Sauser, J., & Shay, A. *Teaching your child racquetball.* Chicago: Contemporary Books, 1978.

Shay, A., & Fancher, T. *40 common errors in racquetball and how to correct them.* Chicago: Contemporary Books, 1978.

Spear, V.I. *Sports Illustrated racquetball.* New York: Lippincott, 1979.

Verner, B., with Skowrup, D. *Racquetball.* Palo Alto, CA: Mayfield, 1977.

Skiing (Alpine)

Evans, H. *We learned to ski.* New York: St. Martin's Press, 1975.

Heller, M., & Godlington, D. *The complete skiing handbook.* New York: Mayflower Books, 1979.

Ski Magazine (Eds.). *Ski Magazine's tips for better skiing.* New York: Harper, 1972.

Ski Magazine (Eds.). *Encyclopedia of skiing.* New York: Harper, 1979.

Skiing (Nordic)

Baldwin, N. *Skiing cross country.* New York: McGraw, 1977.

Caldwell, J. *Cross-country skiing today.* Brattleboro, VT: Greene Press, 1977.

Gillette, N. *Cross-country skiing.* Seattle: Mountaineers, 1979.

Lier, H., & Peterson, H. (Eds.). *I hope I get a purple ribbon.* Brattleboro, VT: United States Ski Association, 1980.

Soccer

Chyzowych, W. *The official soccer book.* Chicago: Rand McNally, 1978.

Ferrell, J. (Ed.). *YMCA Youth Soccer Coaches Manual.* Colorado Springs, CO: National Board of YMCAs, 1980.

Haight, A.L. *The soccer coaching guide.* San Diego: Barnes, 1979.

Ingels, N.B. *Coaching youth soccer.* Palo Alto, CA: Page-Ficklin, 1975.

Ramsay, G., & Harris, P. *The joy of coaching youth soccer.* Manhattan Beach, CA: Soccer for Americans, 1979.

Softball

Brown, P. *Coaching youth softball.* North Palm Beach, FL: Athletic Institute, 1978.

Perry, G.R. *Slow pitch softball.* San Diego: Barnes, 1979.

Walsh, L. *Contemporary softball.* Chicago: Contemporary Books, 1978.

Swimming

Bland, H. *Competitive swimming.* East Ardsley, Wakefield, West Yorkshire, England: E.P. Publishing, 1979.

Colwin, C. *An introduction to swimming coaching: Official course content, level one, National Coaching Certification Program.* Ottawa, Ontario: Canadian Amateur Swimming Association, 1977.

Counsilman, J.E. *Competitive swimming manual for coaches and swimmers.* Bloomington, IN: Counsilman, 1977.

Ryan, F. *Swimming skills: Freestyle, butter-*

fly, backstroke, breaststroke. New York: Penguin, 1978.

Tennis

Braden, V., & Bruns, B. *Teaching children tennis the Vic Braden way.* Boston: Little, Brown, & Co., Sports Illustrated Book, 1980.

Brown, J. *Tennis: Strokes, strategy, and programs.* Englewood Cliffs, NJ: Prentice-Hall, 1980.

Faulkner, E.J., & Weymuller, F. *Ed Faulkner's tennis: How to play it, how to teach it.* New York: Dial, 1970.

Track and Field

Brauman, K. *Handbook of drills and techniques for coaching high school track and field.* West Nyak, NY: Parker, 1979.

Colfer, G. *Handbook for coaching cross country and running events.* West Nyak NY: Parker, 1977.

Robison, C., Jensen, C.R., James, S.W., & Hirschi, W.M. *Modern techniques of track and field.* Philadelphia: Lea & Febiger, 1974.

Volleyball

Cox, R.H. *Teaching volleyball.* Minneapolis: Burgess, 1980.

Robison, B. *Sports Illustrated volleyball.* Philadelphia: Lippincott, 1972.

Scates, A.E. *Winning volleyball* (2nd ed.). Boston: Allyn & Bacon, 1976.

Wrestling

Coaching U.S. kids' wresting. North Palm Beach FL: The Athletic Institute, 1977.

Combs, S., with Frank, C. *Winning wrestling.* Chicago: Contemporary Books, 1980.

Kraft, K. *Mastering wrestling.* Chicago: Contemporary Books, 1977.

Douglas, B. *Wrestling—The making of a champion.* Ithaca, NY: Cornell University Press, 1972.

Keith, A. *The complete guide to championship wrestling.* West Nyak, NY: Parker, 1968.

APPENDIX C

Major Youth Sports Organizations

Archery

National Archery Association
   (target archery)
1750 E. Boulder St.
Colorado Springs, CO 80909
(303)632-5551

National Field Archery Association
   (field archery)
Route 2, P.O. Box 514
Redlands, CA 92373
(714)794-2133

YMCA Youth Sports Development
1750 E. Boulder St.
Colorado Springs, CO 80909
(303)632-5551

Badminton

U.S. Badminton Association
P.O. Box 237
Swartz Creek, MI 48473
(313)655-4502

Baseball

Amateur Athletic Union (AAU)/USA

Junior Olympics
3400 W. 86 St.
Indianapolis, IN 46268
(317)872-2900

American Amateur Baseball Congress
212 Plaza Bldg.
2855 W. Market St.
Akron, OH 44313
(216)836-6424

American Legion Baseball
P.O. Box 1055
Indianapolis, IN 46206
(317)635-8411

Babe Ruth Baseball
1770 Brunswick Ave., P.O. Box 5000
Trenton, NJ 08638
(609)695-1434

George Khoury Association of Baseball
   Leagues
10934 Lin-Valle Dr.
St. Louis, MO 63123
(314)894-1900

Little League Baseball
P.O. Box 3485

Williamsport, PA 17701
(717)326-1921

National Amateur Baseball Federation
2201 N. Townline Rd.
Rose City, MI 48654
(517)685-2990

National Baseball Congress
P.O. Box 1420
338 S. Sycamore
Wichita, KS 67201
(316)267-7333

Pony Baseball
P.O. Box 225
Washington, PA 15301
(412)225-1060

YMCA Youth Sports Development
Address on page 195

Basketball

AAU/USA Junior Olympics
Address on page 195

Little Dribblers Basketball
Alcade Bldg., 518 Ave. H.
Levelland, TX 79336
(806)894-5178

YMCA Youth Sports Development
Address on page 195

Boating

National Association of Amateur Oarsman
4 Boat House Row
Philadelphia, PA 19130
(215)769-2068

Bowling

American Junior Bowling Congress
5301 S. 76 St.
Greendale, WI 53129
(414)421-4700

Cycling

United States Cycling Federation
1750 E. Boulder St.
Colorado Springs, CO 80909
(303)632-5551

Diving

AAU/USA Junior Olympics
Address on page 195

United States Diving, Inc.
3400 W. 86 St.
Indianapolis, IN 46268
(317)872-2900

YMCA Youth Sports Development
Address on page 195

Equestrian

American Horse Shows Association
598 Madison Ave.
New York, NY 10022
(212)759-3070

Fencing

Amateur Fencers League of America
601 Curtis St.
Albany, CA 94706
(415)525-1855

Field Hockey

United States Field Hockey Association
1750 E. Boulder St.
Colorado Springs, CO 80909
(303)632-5551

Football

Pop Warner Junior League Football
   (tackle football)
Suite 606
1315 Walnut St.

Philadelphia, PA 19107
(215)735-1450

YMCA Youth Sports Development
  (flag football)
Address on page 195

Frisbee

International Frisbee Disc Association
P.O. Box 970
San Gabriel, CA 91776
(213)287-2257

Golf

United States Golf Association
Golf House
Far Hills, NJ 07931
(201)234-2300

Gymnastics

AAU/USA Junior Olympics
Address on page 195

United States Gymnastics Federation
P.O. Box 7686
Ft. Worth, TX 76111
(817)485-7630

United States Gymnastics Safety Federation
2349 Emeralo Heights Ct.
Reston, VA 22091
(703)476-6660

YMCA Youth Sports Development
Address on page 195

Handball

United States Handball Association
4101 Dempster St.
Skokie, IL 60076
(312)673-4000

Hockey

Amateur Hockey Association of the United
  States

2997 Broadmoor Valley Rd.
Colorado Springs, CO 80906
(303)576-4990

Judo

AAU/USA Junior Olympics
Address on page 195

United States Judo Association
6417 Manchester Ave.
St. Louis, MO 63139
(314)644-3514

United States Judo Federation
21054 Sarah Hills Dr.
Saratoga, CA 95070
(408)288-9850

YMCA Youth Sports Development
Address on page 195

Racquetball

American Amateur Racquetball Association
5545 Murray Ave.
Memphis, TN 38117
(901)761-1172

United States Racquetball Association
4101 Dempster St.
Skokie, IL 60076
(312)673-4000

YMCA Youth Sports Development
Address on page 195

Rodeo

National Little Britches Rodeo Association
1050 Yuma St. #306
Denver, CO 80204
(303)893-0602

Roller Skating

United States Amateur Confederation of
  Roller Skating
7700 A St.
P.O. Box 83067

Lincoln, NE 68510
(402)483-7551

Shooting

National Rifle Association of America
1600 Rhode Island Ave., N.W.
Washington, DC 20036
(202)828-6000

Skating

Amateur Skating Union of the United States
 (speed skating)
4423 W. Deming Pl.
Chicago, IL 60639
(312)235-9581

Ice Skating Institute of America
1000 Skokie Blvd.
Wilmette, IL 60091
(312)256-5060

United States Figure Skating Association
20 First St.
Colorado Springs, CO 80906
(303)635-5200

Skiing

Bill Koch Ski League
 (cross country skiing)
Box 777
Brattleboro, VT 05301
(802)257-7113

United States Ski Association
P.O. Box 100
Park City, UT 84060
(801)649-9090

Soap Box Derby

All American Soap Box Derby
789 Derby Downs Dr.
Akron, OH 44306
(216)733-8723

Soccer

American Youth Soccer Organization
P.O. Box 5045
Hawthorne, CA 90250
(213)679-1455

Cosmopolitan Soccer League
P.O. Box 1117
Secaucus, NJ 07094
(201)348-8448

Soccer Association for Youth
5945 Ridge Ave.
Cincinnati, OH 45213
(513)351-7291

United States Soccer Federation
350 Fifth Ave., Room 4010
New York, NY 10001
(212)736-0915

YMCA Youth Sports Development
Address on page 195

Softball

Amateur Softball Association of America
2801 N.E. 50th
Oklahoma City, OK 73111
(405)424-5266

YMCA Youth Sports Development
Address on page 195

Squash

United States Squash Racquets Association
211 Ford Rd.
Bala-Cynwyd, PA 19004
(215)667-4006

Surfing

American Surfing Association
P.O. Box 2622
Newport Beach, CA 92663
(213)273-4025

Swimming

AAU/USA Junior Olympics
Address on page 195

United States Swimming, Inc.
1750 E. Boulder St.
Colorado Springs, CO 80909
(303)632-5551

YMCA Youth Sports Development
Address on page 195

Table Tennis

AAU/USA Junior Olympics
Address on page 195

United States Table Tennis Association
1750 E. Boulder St.
Colorado Springs, CO 80909
(303)632-5551

YMCA Youth Sports Development
Address on page 195

Team Handball

United States Team Handball Federation
1750 E. Boulder St.
Colorado Springs, CO 80909
(303)632-5551

YMCA Youth Sports Development
Address on page 195

Tennis

National Junior Tennis League
25 W. 39 St., Suite 1107
New York, NY 10018
(212)869-3322

National Public Park Tennis Association
155 W. Washington Blvd.
Los Angeles, CA 90015
(213)744-4381

United States Tennis Association
Education and Research Center
729 Alexander Rd.

Princeton, NJ 08540
(609)452-2580

YMCA Youth Sports Development
Address on page 195

Track and Field

AAU/USA Junior Olympics
Address on page 195

Track and Field Association of the United
   States of America
10920 Ambassador Dr., Suite 322
Kansas City, MO 64153
(816)891-1077

Twirling

United States Twirling Association
P.O. Box 477
Syracuse, IN 46567
(219)457-3065

Volleyball

AAU/USA Junior Olympics
Address on page 195

United States Volleyball Association
1750 E. Boulder St.
Colorado Springs, CO 80909
(303)632-5551

YMCA Youth Sports Development
Address on page 195

Water Skiing

American Water Ski Association
P.O. Box 191
Winter Haven, FL 33880
(813)324-4341

Wrestling

AAU/USA Junior Olympics
Address on page 195

United States Wrestling Federation
405 W. Hall of Fame

Stillwater, OK 74074
(405)377-5242

YMCA Youth Sports Development
Address on page 195

General
Youth Organizations *

Boys' Clubs of America
771 First Ave.
New York, NY 10017
(212)557-7755

The Sunday School Board of the Southern
   Baptist Convention
Church Recreation Department
127 Ninth Ave. North
Nashville, TN 37234
(615)251-2000

*Sport programs sponsored by these organizations
vary from club to club.

Sports Organizations for
Special Populations

American Athletic Association for the Deaf
3916 Lantern Drive
Silver Spring, MD 20902
(301)942-4042

Healthsports, Inc.
1455 W. Lake St.
Minneapolis, MN 55408
(612)827-3611

National Association of Sports for Cerebral
   Palsied
P.O. Box 3874, Amity Station
New Haven, CT 06525
(203)397-1402

National Foundation of Wheelchair Tennis
3857 Birch St.
Box 411
Newport Beach, CA 92660
(714)851-2277

National Handicapped Sports and
   Recreation Association
P.O. Box 18664
Capital Hills Station
Denver, CO 80218
(303)978-0564

National Wheelchair Athletic Association
40-24 62 St.
Woodside, NY 11377
(212)898-0976

Special Olympics
1701 K St., N.W., Suite 203
Washington, DC 20006
(202)331-1346

United States Association of Blind Athletes
55 W. California Ave.
Beach Haven, NJ 08008
(609)492-1017

United States Deaf Skiers Association
159 Davis Ave.
Hackensack, NJ 07601
(201)489-3777

NOTES

NOTES

NOTES

NOTES

NOTES

NOTES

NOTES

NOTES